Communication Strategies

Communication Strategies

Write your incident communication plan now

Jim Preen

CRISIS SOLUTIONS

BSI

First published in the UK in 2009
by
BSI
389 Chiswick High Road
London W4 4AL

© British Standards Institution 2009

All rights reserved. Except as permitted under the *Copyright, Designs and Patents Act 1988*, no part of this publication may be reproduced, stored in a retrieval system or transmitted in any form or by any means – electronic, photocopying, recording or otherwise – without prior permission in writing from the publisher.

Whilst every care has been taken in developing and compiling this publication, BSI accepts no liability for any loss or damage caused, arising directly or indirectly in connection with reliance on its contents except to the extent that such liability may not be excluded in law.

The right of Jim Preen to be identified as the author of this Work has been asserted by him in accordance with sections 77 and 78 of the *Copyright, Designs and Patents Act 1988*.

Typeset in Frutiger by Helius – www.helius.biz
Printed in Great Britain by Berforts Group. www.berforts.com

British Library Cataloguing in Publication Data
A catalogue record for this book is available from the British Library

ISBN 978-0-580-67621-5

Contents

Introduction ix

1. Types of incidents 1
    Is this serious or are we just having a bad day? 1
    Slow-burn or sudden 1
    Potential risks 3

2. Determining the contents of your plan 7
    Questions you need to ask 7
    Hitting the phone 7
    Where is everybody? 8
    Here's one I prepared earlier 8
    Press conference locations 9
    Fact sheets 9
    Winning the media war 10
    Setting a budget 11
    Recovery site 11
    Evaluation 11

3. Press gang 13
    What will the media want to know? 13
    Unexpected questions 18

4. Strategy layout 19
    Statement of intent 19
    Plan layout 19
    Aide-mémoire 20
    Strategic intent, main effort and the six questions 23
    Incident management team 25

5. How the strategy migrates to a plan 27
    The communications team 27

Contents

The early hours and days	27
What can you expect?	27
Roles and responsibilities	28
Gizmos, gadgets and equipment	34

6. Press conferences — 36
- Theatre — 36
- The venue — 36
- The role of the spokesperson — 38
- The role of the press officer — 40
- Over the internet — 42

7. Holding statements, press releases and templates — 44
- Further plan components — 44

8. Coping with the press pack — 51
- Best practice for dealing with the media — 51
- Interview techniques for both the written and electronic media — 53

9. Media monitoring — 58
- Do we need this? — 58
- In-house monitoring — 58
- Media monitoring report form — 60
- Outsourcing media monitoring — 62

10. Call-takers — 64
- Who is calling please? — 64
- Pre-prepared responses for call-takers — 64
- Stressful times call for cool heads — 65
- Templates — 65
- Getting the information to the right people — 69
- What callers hate — 69

11. Information, fact sheets and general know-how — 70
- A grab bag of ideas — 70

Contents

Key contacts	70
Call cascade	70
Stakeholder contacts	71
Press kits	71
Incident website	72
Fact sheets	72
Recovery site	73
Past incidents and emergencies	74
Battle box	76
12. Post-incident evaluation	**78**
Now can we forget about that?	78
Stakeholders – how do they feel about your organization now?	79
13. Testing the plan	**85**
So does the plan work?	85
Types of exercises	85
Simple exercises	87
Medium exercises	87
Complex exercises	88
Aims and objectives	88
Who do you want to involve?	89
Planners	89
Case study	90
How the teams fared	96
Action plan	97
I want to stage a similar exercise – is there anything else I need to know?	97
14. Communication plan checklist	**99**
Time to get cracking	99
References	**102**

Introduction

A colleague at Crisis Solutions once said that in most cases managing an incident is essentially the same as managing the media. Some people may not agree, but the truth is that if you do not deal quickly and effectively with the media fallout from an incident then your troubles may have only just begun.

This book should be read in conjunction with *BS 25999-1:2006, Business continuity management: Code of practice*, which establishes the principles of business continuity management. The standard sets out the requirement for a communication plan and is the starting point for this book.

Most organizations need a plan – even HM Revenue & Customs (HMRC). I should know because a few years ago, I wrote a communication plan for HMRC that involved travelling around the country to several of their offices, looking at disaster recovery sites and interviewing numerous members of staff. A process that anyone writing such a plan will have to undertake.

But this book is not just about communicating with the media – it has a wider remit; for example, on one occasion a client remarked that even if the world's press were banging on the door, he would want to let his staff know what was going on first, before talking to journalists. So we will also look at internal communications – what to say to your staff. But bear in mind that whatever you do say to your staff may up in the media, so consistent messages must be employed.

The media is fond of playing divide and rule so if you say one thing to your staff and another to the press – particularly if they are contradictory – then reporters will pursue you.

Media monitoring

Those working in communications generally take a keen interest in the news. As we will see, media monitoring during an incident is of prime importance – how will you know if you are winning the media war if you do not know what the press are saying about you?

Introduction

During an incident, it is essential that the communications team learn to think like journalists – only then will they be able to anticipate a reporter's actions and questions.

As a former political reporter, Alistair Campbell, former Prime Minister Tony Blair's press secretary, had an astute take on managing the media. Campbell instituted The Grid which itemized all upcoming events – both good and bad – putting his press room completely across the news cycle and allowing them to get their retaliation in first. He always maintained a critical story needed a full stop to draw it to a close – that or time – and claimed that only huge stories ran for more than 11 days.

Is this a story?

So what does constitute news? Lord Northcliffe – the press baron – famously said, 'News is what someone, somewhere is trying to suppress, the rest is just advertising'. To me this still has the ring of truth about it.

People not in the media often assume the news is just 'what happens', but as any journalist will tell you, hours are spent in newsrooms with people saying, 'Is this news? Will anyone care about this story?'. Similarly what is big news one day may be spiked the next. And of course if your organization is undergoing an incident you may be hoping for a larger story to come along to knock you out of the headlines.

In 1997 several other journalists and I were told to prepare to fly to India because it was widely known that Mother Teresa was very ill and would probably die in the next few days. Just prior to leaving, Princess Diana was killed in a car crash in Paris. Mother Teresa did indeed die, but I never went to India as what would under normal circumstances have been a front-page story was virtually ignored as the Princess's death reverberated around the world. Predicting what will lead the news is a tricky business.

The public mood – ignore it at your peril

One of the main themes in this book is the importance of keeping in touch with the public mood. If your actions do not reflect the thoughts and feelings of your staff, clients, customers or indeed the wider public then your communications strategy is not working.

Introduction

To give an example, when terrorists attacked London on 7 July 2005 the emergency services took a long time to set up an emergency phone number for those trying to find information about family and friends.

When the number was finally broadcast, switchboards were immediately swamped with calls – people were left hanging on the phone for long periods of time – only to discover later that this was not a freephone line but was costing, in some instances, up to 50p a minute.

Getting it right

But I do not want to accentuate only the negative – what about getting it right?

On the same day, Ken Livingstone, then the Mayor of London, issued a statement that I would argue got it spectacularly right. In the opening few paragraphs he praised the emergency services for their work and Londoners for their calm response – all essential details – but then he made what could have been a bland political statement come alive.

Here is part of what he had to say:

> *I want to say one thing specifically to the world today. This was not a terrorist attack against the mighty and the powerful. It was not aimed at Presidents or Prime Ministers. It was aimed at ordinary, working-class Londoners, black and white, Muslim and Christian, Hindu and Jew, young and old. It was an indiscriminate attempt to slaughter, irrespective of any considerations for age, for class, for religion, or whatever.*
>
> *That isn't an ideology, it isn't even a perverted faith – it is just an indiscriminate attempt at mass murder and we know what the objective is. They seek to divide Londoners. They seek to turn Londoners against each other. Londoners will not be divided by this cowardly attack. They will stand together in solidarity alongside those who have been injured and those who have been bereaved and that is why I'm proud to be the mayor of that city.*

In my view, the Mayor's choice of words and his tone were entirely appropriate and in touch with the public mood.

Naturally, any communication plan must contain pre-prepared press statements and these will be examined in detail.

Introduction

Writing your plan

There are many excellent books available on incident or crisis communications – where this book differs is that it is an attempt to outline all that is needed to create a communication plan. It is not a plan in itself and contains far more detail than most plans require. Think of it as a set of building blocks – take what you need, construct the plan that meets your requirements and discard the rest.

A plan must be user-friendly, should be compressed, flexible and easy to use. Huge screeds of text won't do – you will need headlines, subheadings and checklists because if you do not include these then your plan may go unread and all your hard work will have been for nothing.

The first part of any communication plan will almost certainly contain a checklist of all the things that must be done now, or at least as soon as the plan is invoked. For many with expertise in communications it will be something of an aide-mémoire. Thereafter we will look at what constitutes an incident press room, what roles need to be filled, what potential crises might beset your organization and what you need to put in place to recover quickly.

We will look at press conferences – how to stage them, the role of press officers and the role of those giving the press conference. We will also look at how to conduct interviews – what to say and what to avoid. In large international organizations, it may well be that the plan will need details of overseas offices. You have a plant in Australia and an incident arises there – who speaks to the press, your staff and customers? There is a 12-hour time difference so waiting for Europe to wake up may not be an option.

In effect fact sheets may have to be written that deal with your various offices, plants, and manufacturing sites both locally and overseas.

Case studies

As well as writing plans I also run courses that help organizations update or institute communication plans. The courses are usually made up of communication experts from across Europe and I often feel that I learn as much as I teach – they tend to be very collaborative sessions.

The courses inevitably employ case studies, quite often these are not detailed expositions but rather brief memorable examples used to back up a particular

Introduction

point. The same is true here, but also included are a couple of full-blown case studies. Every effort has been made to keep examples fresh and modern and not to trot out those that are familiar. Often they are instances of things I witnessed when working as a journalist.

BS 25999

Subclause 8.5.5 of BS 25999 has this to say about communications:

The organization's media response should be documented in the IMP [incident management plan], including:

a) the incident communications strategy;
b) the organization's preferred interface with the media;
c) a guideline or template for the drafting of a statement to be provided to the media at the earliest practicable opportunity following the incident;
d) appropriate numbers of trained, competent, spokespeople nominated and authorized to release information to the media;
e) establishment, where practicable, of a suitable venue to support liaison with the media, or other stakeholder groups.

In some cases, it may be appropriate to:

- *provide supporting detail in a separate document;*
- *establish an appropriate number of competent, trained people to answer telephone enquiries from the press;*
- *prepare background material about the organization and its operations (this information should be pre-agreed for release);*
- *ensure that all media information is made available without undue delay.*

The commentary on 8.5.5 goes on to say:

Pre-prepared information can be especially useful in the early stages of an incident. It enables an organization to provide details about the organization and its business while details of the incident are still being established. An organization may use all applicable means to share information during and after an incident. Such sources may include websites, spokespeople, news sources, and generic company briefing statements.

8.5.6   This subclause deals with stakeholder management:

Introduction

A process for identifying and prioritizing communications with other key stakeholders should be included. It may be necessary to develop a separate stakeholder management plan to provide criteria for setting priorities and allocating a person to each stakeholder or group of stakeholders.

And, tellingly, the commentary on 8.5.6 makes the point:

Pressure or community action groups who collectively have power or influence over the organization might also need to be considered.

If journalists can cause your organization trouble, then journalists in conjunction with activists and pressure groups can open the door to a whole world of pain.

I have quoted the relevant subclauses of BS 25999 in some detail because although they are brief, circumscribed and to the point, to be able to respond in the manner they suggest means a lot of hard work and attention to detail. The Standard must remain our watchword throughout this book, which will only be judged a success if it enables you and your organization to comply more readily with BS 25999 and thus be well prepared to deal with incidents.

One thing I have noticed over the years, whether during real crises or simulations, is that there is quite often a strong individual communicator – usually the head of communications – who takes control of the situation. A real worry for many organizations is: what if that individual is ill, away on holiday or leaves the company? The beauty of having a communication plan is that if it is correctly researched and written it should work regardless of who is in charge.

Keeping it fresh

Once a plan is written, someone has to take ownership of it.

A call cascade has been described as 'tool number one' in an incident media toolkit, but what use is a call cascade if it is not kept up to date? Someone must grasp that responsibility and indeed the responsibility for keeping the whole plan current.

Finally, once it is complete, do not let your plan gather cyberdust on your computer's hard drive. If you have done a good job then shout it from the rooftops and let people know. And do not just send your colleagues an email attachment of your work. Email attachments have a remarkable ability to go

Introduction

unread. Print copies and distribute them, then hold half-day sessions to introduce staff to the plan.

One of the great gripes within the business continuity fraternity is getting senior management buy in. Senior executives do not like the look of crises and usually do not wish to be reminded of them. They can also be a little hesitant when it comes to opening the chequebook to pay for matters related to incident planning.

Well the good news is that writing a communication plan will cost very little aside from the time spent putting it together. If you have been tasked with writing or updating such a plan then read on.

1. Types of incidents

'When people talk, listen completely. Most people never listen.'
Ernest Hemingway

Is this serious or are we just having a bad day?

In communications terms you are involved in an incident if the reputation of your organization is threatened – usually as a result of hostile media attention. Many factors can contribute to an incident, but if you or your company are perceived to be to blame for what has occurred then your problems are likely to intensify – we live in a blame culture.

If a terror bomb detonates outside your offices, you cannot be held responsible even if you are the target of the attack – you are not to blame. But if your response to the situation is deemed to be slow or inept, then your reputation could be threatened.

Slow-burn or sudden

Emergencies are often thought of as bolts from the blue – something unforeseen and unexpected. That is not always true. In general it is possible to identify two types of incident: a sudden or abrupt incident and what can be called a slow-burn incident.

The first is the bolt from the blue – perhaps a plane crash or a terror attack. There will be little time to plan for such an event so a communication plan that sets out roles, responsibilities and tasks is essential. It may be difficult to contact staff in such circumstances, so a call-out plan or call cascade will be an indispensable tool.

The second type can be called a slow-burn incident – for example, a major strike or outbreak of disease. It is possible to see these incidents coming, but of course their severity and duration may be unpredictable. It should be possible, however, to tailor a plan to deal with such an event.

Before starting to write a communication plan you will need to carry out a communications risk assessment on behalf of your organization. Specific areas

Types of incidents

of your plan will need to reflect where you are most at risk. If you are an airline then your plan will need to contain pre-prepared press releases in the event of a plane crash. Similarly if you are in heavy industry and part of your plant can be dangerous your plan will need to contain details such as the plant's safety record and your operating procedures together with press release templates.

Memorable example

Lockerbie air crash

If you are a victim of a terror attack this may cause your company serious problems and you will need to have a business continuity plan all set to go to overcome the emergency. It should not, however, cause you a problem with the media unless the problem is of your own making. If you are seen to be inept, insensitive or out of touch with the public mood, the media and the public may turn against you.

It is always astonishing when leading companies go out of business – they seem to be part of the international business architecture – but where are Pan Am and, more recently, Lehman Brothers? What seemed bulletproof companies are no longer trading.

In the case of Pan Am, the company was the victim of a dreadful terror attack when Flight 103 fell out of the sky onto a Scottish village killing all 259 passengers and 11 crew on 21 December 1988. The plane was half an hour from Heathrow Airport, where it had picked up 49 passengers from a connecting flight from Frankfurt.

The US embassy in Europe had received a warning concerning a possible bomb threat to a Pan Am flight from Frankfurt to the US two weeks before the attack on Flight 103 took place. Although the press initially concentrated on the human loss, they wanted to know very quickly not only which terrorist group was responsible but also how the bomb had got onto the plane in the first place.

Pan Am said little. When the company did make a statement, it claimed there had been no bomb warning, and chief executive officer (CEO) Thomas Plaskett lay low and said nothing. He did not visit the site or attend the victims' funerals – he was effectively invisible.

Types of incidents

> The aftermath of what had begun as a heartbreaking human story saw the unravelling of the company. Passengers abandoned Pan Am and the company folded. This might have happened anyway, but the actions or rather inactions of the company and its CEO may have helped speed them down that course.

Potential risks

Here are examples of potential risks that could affect your organization:

- Terror attack
- Plane crash
- Disease outbreak
- Loss of critical data
- IT crash that involves data loss
- Product recall
- Outsourced products that bear your name prove to be faulty or in some way reflect badly on your organization
- Staff or other company stakeholders die or are injured
- Hostile takeover bid
- Illness caused by your company that affects the general public (release of toxic gases, chemical spill, food poisoning, etc)
- Death of top executive
- Floods/earthquake/other severe weather
- Fire or explosion at your plant/factory/offices, etc.
- Your company is associated with some form of fraud or embezzlement
- Major interruption to your business operation (strikes, illness, loss of power/data)
- A change in the law making some part of your operation illegal or at best out of step with public opinion
- Share price plummeting
- Significant job losses
- Closing of a plant/factory/office
- Senior executive caught lying or at least being 'economical with the truth'
- Senior member of your company involved in a personal scandal
- Senior executive inadvertently says damaging things about your organization.

Types of incidents

Some of these incidents are entirely unpredictable – some are not. Where is your company most at risk? Talk to your colleagues, find out more and keep a list.

Before we move on, what about the last bullet point: senior executive inadvertently says damaging things about your organization? That sounds familiar.

Memorable example

Doing a Ratner

Many people in the UK will the know the story of jewellery boss Gerald Ratner calling one of his products 'crap', which led to the rapid unravelling of his firm and his fortune. Whenever a senior executive says something less than complimentary about their firm (for example, when an executive at Topman said their target market was 'hooligans' whose suits would be 'worn at his first job interview or first court case!') it is now known as 'doing a Ratner' and his story is dutifully wheeled out.

In his autobiography[1] Ratner makes the point, 'I had worked bloody hard for 30 years, making millions of pounds for shareholders and creating thousands of jobs for a company I loved, and I had suddenly had it taken away from me. Not for doing anything criminal. I hadn't embezzled. I hadn't lied. All I had done was say a sherry decanter was crap'. In monetary terms he lost a £650,000 salary, had £500 million wiped off the valuation of his company and as he says, 'a billion-pound turnover slashed overnight'.

A common fear among those facing the media is that they will say something off the cuff or spontaneous that under normal circumstances they would never dream of saying, or that their words will be twisted by unscrupulous journalists to mean something they never intended.

A common misconception is that Ratner made an unscripted remark, which he was to regret later. In fact he had made the remark about the sherry decanter being crap many times before – his other favourite gag was to say that some of Ratners' earrings were cheaper than a Marks & Spencer prawn sandwich. His intention was clear – to be funny in a self-deprecating way.

Types of incidents

> In 1991 he was asked to speak at an Institute of Directors (IoD) annual conference being held at the Royal Albert Hall. Clearly this was a wealthy group of people who had probably never bought any of Ratners' high street jewellery. He made the jokes, got a laugh and a standing ovation at the end of the speech.
>
> Let us pause and leave Ratner, with the applause ringing in his ears.

This book is not given much to theory, but when talking to the media the experience can be divided into three component parts: the Medium, the Message and the Audience.

The Medium is the method by which it is transmitted (radio, newspaper, television, etc), the Message or messages are the points you want to get across during the interview and, finally, the Audience are those people who hear or read your words. All are important, but the audience stands head and shoulders above the other two.

> Let us return to Ratner. As he leaves the Royal Albert Hall a journalist from the *Daily Mirror* accosts him and asks why he is knowingly selling crap to his customers. The next day the headline in *The Sun* was 'Crapners' and the *Daily Mirror* went with 'You 22 carat gold mugs'. Ratner's great mistake was in thinking he was merely talking to the audience in front of him – in this case members of the IoD. Of course with journalists and camera crews present, his remarks went a lot further than he had anticipated.
>
> *The Sun,* in particular, went after him even when he had to sell his house, which of course became known as 'the house that crap built'. Some messages work for some audiences and others do not. The IoD audience laughed and *The Sun,* on behalf of its readers, took a po-faced attitude that affects Ratner to this day.

When journalists are present always assume that the microphone is on, the camera is turning and the notebook is open, and make sure your messages are in tune with all of your audiences – particularly those not present.

Communication Strategies

Types of incidents

> ## *What have I learned from this chapter?*
>
> - There are two types of incident – sudden impact and slow-burn
> - I need to identify areas where my organization is at risk
> - These risk areas must be reflected in my plan
> - Do not call any of your products 'crap'.

2. Determining the contents of your plan

'Be sincere, be brief, be seated.' Franklin Delano Roosevelt

Questions you need to ask

Before starting to write a communication plan ask yourself and others what needs to be included. Do not worry if you do not have all the answers to the questions – right now it is the questions that are important. The answers can follow later.

First of all, who are you going to need in an incident press room and how will it differ, if at all, from your usual communications team? What roles and responsibilities need to be taken care of? Will roles change significantly because of an emergency?

Hitting the phone

Will you need more people than usual? Do not forget the phone is likely to be ringing off the hook. Who is going to take those calls? Perhaps you have a public relations (PR) agency that can help or perhaps you need to bring people in from other departments? But if you do that there could be problems, as many will have never dealt with journalists and anxious or angry members of the public before.

Some form of template is going to be required for those taking calls from journalists, staff and other stakeholders. What should be contained within these templates? Do you or your senior press people want to be answering the phone all the time or are some of the team better placed dealing with strategy rather than jumping at every phone that rings?

And talking of phones, they tend to play a significant role in an emergency – you may find that all your lines are constantly engaged to the point where it is hard to get a call out. Do you know how to arrange for extra lines to be fed into your communications room? You may also need to set up an emergency phone line for colleagues, families and friends who are looking for updated information. Do you know how to set up an emergency number? And if you do who will answer the calls or will it be a recorded message?

Determining the contents of your plan

Where is everybody?

Still on the subject of phones, their most important function may be in finding and assembling your team. Do you have a call-out system or at least a contact list of all your people? Is the list up to date?

If you use or are considering using a call-cascade system, is it in place and has it been tested? Some companies use a system based on SMS text messaging. But do not forget in a major emergency (for example, the 7 July 2005 bombing in London) mobile phones may not work for many hours.

Incidents have an irritating habit of happening out of office hours. Is there a duty press officer who has a phone and can initiate a call cascade or who at least has a current contacts list? How do you gain access to your office outside of office hours?

And of course it is not just the press that will be calling. What about staff and their families – who will be communicating with them? Do you need a dedicated internal communications team?

And what about customers and other stakeholders – how will their needs be addressed? Who will be figuring out 'lines to take' and the messages that need to be transmitted? Who signs off on these messages? Speed of response is essential in the opening minutes and hours of an incident. You may have a perfect press release ready to go but if it has to be signed off by someone who cannot be found, what do you do then?

Here's one I prepared earlier

What about pre-prepared press statements? They could save time at the start of an incident, but what should they say? Who is going to talk to the press, who is going to give interviews? Who is going to decide whether it is a good idea to give interviews? If it is your CEO who will talk to the press, have they received media training, are they comfortable with this responsibility? What happens if they are sick or away, who speaks then? Speaking to a hostile press during an incident is vastly different to delivering company results at an AGM (annual general meeting).

If the incident is taking place overseas, should the CEO travel to the incident or is it best for them to stay at headquarters (HQ)? If that is the case do you need a

Determining the contents of your plan

spokesperson to travel to the site? Who is that person and have they received media training? What about a press liaison person at the scene of the incident – who will fulfil that role and what are their responsibilities?

Press conference locations

At some point you may need to hold a press conference – do you have a location in mind? It might be easier for your CEO to conduct a press conference at your offices, but do you really want journalists on your premises during an incident? Are there hotels or conference centres that you could use? If so, what is their capacity? How much do they cost? Can they be booked at short notice?

Who needs to be informed at the start of an incident? Senior management and the communications team, clearly, but what about other people – who needs to be kept informed? For example, what about your receptionist? The receptionist would need to know where calls should be sent. Should families and friends be switched through to the communications room or should they go to human resources (HR)? Also, if a pack of journalists suddenly appear at your HQ, your receptionist won't thank you if they know nothing of the unfolding incident – leaving them ill-prepared and taken aback.

Fact sheets

In normal times you probably deal with journalists on a regular basis who know a great deal about your organization. This will most likely not be the case during a significant incident. Journalists will be calling who know little or nothing of what you do. Do you have facts and figures about your organization available? Where are they held and are they current? How will you transmit this information?

When time is precious you do not want to be repeating the same information time and again. Clearly some form of press kit needs to be prepared, but what should it contain, where should it be held and who has responsibility for keeping it up to date? For example, if aircraft form part of your business you will need to have details as to types of plane, cruising speeds, safety record, number of miles safely flown, etc.

During an emergency you may have to deal with the emergency services – who will liaise with the police? If the police give a press conference during the course

Determining the contents of your plan

of the incident they may ask you to attend. Is this a good idea? What criteria do you need to consider when deciding whether or not to attend?

If people have been taken to hospital who will liaise with the hospital authorities?

How will you protect the injured and their families from press intrusion?

> ### *Memorable example*
>
> #### Looking after those left behind
>
> In the immediate aftermath of the Lockerbie air crash, friends and family members who travelled to the site had to walk past the many journalists assembled at the scene. In large numbers, journalists can be extremely intimidating. Questions were shouted, cameras rolled and flashguns popped – not a comfortable situation for those who had just lost loved ones.
>
> By contrast after the Concorde crash in Paris in 2000, relatives and friends were kept well away from the press. They were put up in a hotel, which was immediately made out of bounds to the media until they had checked in. Thereafter their progress was strictly monitored by the authorities who kept the media at bay.

Winning the media war

What about media monitoring? How will you know you are conducting a successful media compaign if you don't know what the press are saying about you? How can you prepare your CEO to face the press if you do not know what is currently in the public domain?

Who will have the time to monitor the media? Could this task be outsourced to a PR company or could you bring in members of other departments to perform this task? If you do you will likely need pre-prepared templates for staff to use as they scan the news media. What should such a template look like?

And talking of PR companies, if you use one, have arrangements been made so that representatives know what is expected of them during an incident? An

Determining the contents of your plan

emergency is no time to discover that a job or task you thought had been outsourced is just not getting done.

Setting a budget

Unfortunately, emergencies cost money – extra staff, facilities and equipment may be needed. What about setting up a contingency budget ahead of time? An incident may not be the best time to be requesting the accounts department for extra funds.

When it comes to writing the plan, how will senior executives be brought on board to endorse and buy into the plan? Writing a plan should not cost vast sums, but time is money so once again a budget needs to be sought.

Recovery site

What happens if you have a major fire or your offices are inaccessible for some other reason? Do you have a recovery site? Do you know where it is and what equipment it contains? Does it have enough computers, phones and video conferencing equipment? Can your IT be switched to your recovery site? Where is all this information held? Do you have 24/7 access?

During the early stages of an incident how will you gather information? Some form of situation report will be called for. What needs to be contained within a situation report? Do you have a template to help draft such a report?

In the aftermath of an incident it is highly likely you will need an audit trail to show how your team performed. A note-taker will be required to itemize what decisions were taken and when so as to provide a complete history of the event. Who fills this role and what are their responsibilities?

Evaluation

The media can be a useful resource for getting information out to the general public. How can this be achieved? Is it part of employees' contracts that they must not talk to the press? Have staff been briefed on what to do if journalists approach them? When an incident is over there should be some form of evaluation as to how both your staff and the communication plan performed. How can this evaluation be best achieved?

Determining the contents of your plan

Finally, a plan is never complete; people join and leave organizations, contact details change, CEOs are replaced, offices are opened and closed, and new products are manufactured. So once a plan is written, who will keep it up to date? How will it be distributed and how will you introduce people to its contents?

If a plan is well written then someone reading it for the first time should be able to use it with ease and confidence, but clearly it is highly desirable that all communications team members and executives should have read and understood the plan prior to an incident taking place. Not least of all because the team may have some excellent suggestions as to how it could be improved.

There may be many other questions that need to be asked prior to writing a plan, many of which will depend on your type of business. Hopefully this chapter has helped formalize your ideas to get you started.

> ### *What have I learned from this chapter?*
>
> The major questions to be asked prior to writing a communication plan are as follows:
>
> - What roles and responsibilities are required within an incident communications team?
> - How will members of the incident communications room be assembled?
> - Who will speak to the press?
> - Who will undertake media monitoring?
> - Who will answer the phones?

3. Press gang

'If I am to speak for ten minutes, I need a week for preparation; if fifteen minutes, three days; if half an hour, two days; if an hour, I am ready now.'
Woodrow Wilson

What will the media want to know?

In the first two chapters we looked at the potential risks and threats that organizations can suffer as well as the questions that need to be asked before commencing to write a plan.

Another way of examining where a company might be at risk and what you need to have in place to mitigate that risk is to don your reporter's hat and consider what questions journalists will ask during an incident.

Here we divide the questions into five categories:

- People
- Description of the incident
- Causes
- Rescue and recovery
- Consequences.

People

Take a look at any newspaper or just about any television news report and ultimately the story will be about people. At the time of writing this book the world is consumed with the financial meltdown, and while there are facts, figures, charts and speculation as to what will become of the world's economy, the underlying story is how this will impact on people. How many will lose their jobs and their homes? Stories about people populate the news.

So when dealing with the press during an incident people must be your priority, as they will certainly be the media's priority. If you seem to care more for your business or your property than for people you will be deemed to be completely out of touch with the public mood, making you an easy target for the press.

Press gang

> ### *Memorable example*
>
> 'A good day to bury bad news?'[2]
>
> At 2.55 p.m. on 11 September 2001, as millions of people were watching the television images of the attacks on the Twin Towers in New York, an email was sent from the Department of Transport in London. The email read, 'It is now a very good day to get out anything we want to bury'. Jo Moore, a Labour Party special adviser or spin doctor, wrote the email and was condemned by a relative of one of the victims for attempting to bury bad news 'under the bodies of 6,500 people'.
>
> Nothing could make press officers or PR advisers look worse. There is little evidence that trying to hide bad news beneath larger stories works. The news media is a large and voracious beast and will seek out new stories, with the result in the case of Moore being that she gave precisely the wrong advice. She appeared crass and insensitive and ultimately drew attention to herself, her minister and to the very information she was trying to bury.
>
> And what was the information she was trying to 'bury'? It was a minor government U-turn on pension rights for councillors. But because of the contents of that one email, she lost her job and so did the Minister for Transport, Stephen Byers.

So in the event of an incident where it looks as if there could be casualties or fatalities, journalists will be asking how many people have been killed, how many are injured and if people are still missing.

As for casualties, journalists will want to know the nature of their injuries, how serious they are and whether any are life threatening. Journalists will often try to get the names of victims, but remember it is the job of the police to release the names of those who have died. Family members do not want to learn about the death of a loved one through the media.

The media will also be asking where the injured and the dead have been taken. If there is a suspicion that a senior member of the organization has died or is missing this will of course be of extreme interest.

Press gang

Initially, at least, you may not want to reveal all this information, but as part of your situation report these facts will have to be gathered, whether it be from your own security people, your colleagues or the emergency services.

On a positive note, the press will also be interested in the survivors – those who got away. Once again if that is someone of prominence it will be of interest and might be something you would be happy to release to the media.

Description of the incident

At the same time as journalists are asking about people caught up in the incident they will also be asking for simple descriptions as to what is going on and what has happened. Are the emergency services on site? Is the building on fire? Where has the plane come down? Are there blasts and explosions? Can you see the incident from where you are? Can you describe what is going on?

They will also be trying to get a sense of the extent of the emergency. How bad is this? At the same time as calling you, reporters will be calling the emergency services so do not attempt to play things down too much as you will appear at odds with what the police are saying, which could open up a whole new area of questioning that might be extremely uncomfortable:

'What do you mean this is nothing? The police are calling it a major incident and the fire service has 50 fire-fighters at the scene – have you not grasped the seriousness of what is going on?'

They will also begin to ask about the estimated value of loss – will the organization be able to continue as a result of the incident? Are there plans in place to deal with such an incident? Will you be forced to transfer your operation elsewhere? If so, do you have other premises?

Reporters will also want to know what the duration of the incident might be and the subsequent consequences to the organization involved. For example, 'It looks like this incident is going to take weeks to be resolved, how are you going to survive and what are you telling your staff and customers?' They will almost certainly ask if you are insured against such loss and whether such an event was foreseeable.

Another line of questioning may focus on the impact of the emergency on other organizations close by. In effect, will your incident be a cause of concern for

Press gang

others? Reporters may also be interested in whether many people witnessed the event and what crowd-control measures were in place, though inevitably these are questions best directed at the police.

Many companies have procedures laid out as to how their work/manufacturing should be carried out. Journalists will inevitably ask what those procedures are and if they were followed. If they have not been followed then there is another opportunity for journalists to start playing the blame game.

Causes

Hard on the heels of questions concerning people and enquiries about what is going on will come the questions about the causes of the incident. What caused it and who is to blame?

As has already been mentioned, if you are responsible for the incident and are seen to be culpable then the media will focus on this aspect of the story.

An incident is almost certainly the worst possible time to have to face the press, but it is also the most important time to do so. An organization at the centre of an emergency has to be seen by the media as the major source of information concerning the story. If the media senses the organization is clamming up then an 'information gap' starts to open up and journalists will go elsewhere in search of a story. They may seek out people who do not have the company's best interests at heart, such as a former employee or perhaps competitors who would be happy to talk you down. Of course reporters may do this anyway, but the only tried and trusted way of getting your side of the story across is to make yourself available to the press – a steady drip-feed of information is the best way to go.

Journalists will be asking for testimony from witnesses – perhaps you could consider putting someone forward. The media and the public are fond of personal stories as they often bring incidents to life and inevitably seem much more human and direct.

The media will want to know who sounded the alarm, who called the emergency services and if there had been previous warnings concerning the incident. In other words, could the incident have been avoided in some way?

Press gang

Press officers, by the nature of their job, should have a good sense of what will play well with the media and the wider public. This expertise should help to determine what can be released to the media and when.

Rescue and recovery

Journalists and their audiences will always be interested in the rescue and recovery elements of a story. Many of these kinds of questions will be directed at the emergency services, but they are also questions you will want to keep on top of.

Reporters will want to know how many people were involved in the rescue and relief, what equipment was used and what has happened to those who have been rescued (what hospital they have been taken to and what condition they are in).

Typically, day two of a story plays out along the lines of 'heroes and villains'. The search is on for those who caused the incident (villains), those who helped to save lives ('have-a-go-heroes') or those who helped in some way to relieve the situation or prevent the incident from getting worse.

If a member of your staff clearly falls into the latter category then, with their permission, the story can be given to the press.

Consequences

The previous categories have dealt with media questions in the immediate aftermath of an event. Many of the questions that follow have to do with events that take place as the story plays out over a matter of days, weeks and months.

Depending on the type of event, reporters may want to ask about stress levels of the survivors and their families. They may be interested in what your organization is doing to help such victims. Are counsellors being made available? Have those caught up in events received sufficient medical treatment? They may also want to talk about the insurance claim if there is one. Has it been paid, has it been delayed?

If people have died there may be inquests, and remember that a year after the event has taken place, if it is of sufficient interest, the anniversary will be recalled

Press gang

and will feature in the press. This is your opportunity to show that you have recovered and moved on – if, of course, that is the case.

There may also be lawsuits and allegations of professional negligence that result from the incident. It is up to the press office to keep track of all of this and to have noted when the court cases are taking place so press releases are ready and company spokespeople are prepared.

Unexpected questions

There may also be times when a reporter calls about something of which you know, or have heard, nothing. With the proliferation of blogs, mobile-phone cameras and so-called citizen journalists, no matter how good your media monitoring, stories and pictures may slip through the net.

If the questions are hostile, it is time to keep a cool head – do not be pressured into answering questions. The best course of action is to get as much information out of the journalist as possible, say you have no comment now but will get back to them shortly with answers. Do not forget journalists have deadlines; if you say you will call back the best advice is to do so.

Finally, there will be the questions constantly asked by the press during an incident:

- When will you be putting out a press release?
- When will you be making a statement?
- When will you be holding a press conference?
- Who will you be putting up for interview?

What have I learned from this chapter?

- Expect questions to be asked about people
- Do not let an information gap open up – talk to the media
- Do not forget the anniversary of the event.

---

4. Strategy layout

'If we want things to stay as they are, things will have to change.'
Giuseppe di Lampedusa

Statement of intent

A communications strategy should start with a statement of intent and thereafter act as an aide-mémoire to help staff to cope with the opening hours of an incident. A statement of intent might look something like this:

Sample statement of intent

For the company to recover from an incident and protect its staff, business and reputation, it must conduct a successful communications strategy. To achieve this the company must:

- Communicate effectively with staff, customers and suppliers
- Maintain proactive and effective relations with the media
- Be open, honest and even-handed with the media
- Keep in touch with the public mood
- Assign roles and responsibilities to employees.

It is also highly desirable to have the organization's CEO or another senior executive endorse the plan to show that it is accepted and approved at the highest level. A signed endorsement at the beginning of the plan should make clear that it is a valuable document that sets out how staff and other stakeholders can be protected during an emergency, while also maintaining the company's reputation.

Plan layout

For a plan to work effectively it needs to be simple and straightforward to use. If it is too bulky or laden with information people will just not look at it. Even useful information can be detrimental if it is provided in the wrong place or in too much detail.

Strategy layout

During an incident people often say they are starved of information – in fact it is often the case that there is too much information, with the additional problem being that it is the wrong kind of information. But, of course, for a plan to be useful it will need to contain important data – some of it quite detailed – and it is where it is placed that counts.

To that purpose the front end of a communications strategy should be largely a series of bullet points indicating actions to be taken or considered. One action point might be: 'Release holding statement or press release'.

Now, contained within the plan there must be examples of pre-prepared press releases and themes that will need to be deployed, but if you keep these in the front end of your plan it is likely there will be a huge amount of detail you do not need that will get in the way of the action points. These details should be contained in easily accessible appendices at the back of the plan.

So, for example, an action point might be: 'Consider holding a press conference (see Appendix 4: How to run a successful press conference)'. A version of the plan is likely to be held on a computer where hyperlinks can be used to take the reader straight to the appendices. In paper form a list of contents should do the job.

The important principle is to keep the front end of the plan simple and straightforward and to put more detailed facts into readily accessible sections at the back.

Aide-mémoire

Those who are writing a plan and indeed those caught up in an incident who have need of a plan may well have a degree of experience of dealing with the press and will often have at least some sense of what is required of them during an incident.

But of course it may just be that the person in need of a communication plan in an emergency may have had nothing to do with writing the plan, may have little experience of dealing with the press in testing circumstances and may have only recently joined the company. This is where an aide-mémoire is required; it is for the old hands and the new hands too.

The aide-mémoire is divided into three sections:

Strategy layout

- Alert
- Prepare to communicate
- Media monitoring.

Alert

Emergencies, by their nature, are stressful and will frequently pull people in several directions at once – simple checklists should help to keep those involved on track. In the early minutes and hours of an incident it is essential to know precisely what is going on. Facts must be gathered and the situation assessed. Although the two may overlap it may be helpful to think in terms of two discrete situation reports: an incident report and a status report.

An incident report will ask many of the same questions that journalists would ask when a story breaks:

- What happened? (Brief statement of facts as known)
- Where? (Location of incident)
- When? (Indication of when incident started)
- How? (Brief description of events leading up to incident)
- Who? (Summary of who is involved)
- What is the immediate impact?
- What is being done? (Clear statement of actions being taken)
- What help is needed?

Thereafter a status report should help to answer the following questions:

- What are the facts as known?
- What is the level of impact/how serious is this?
- Should the incident communication plan be activated?
- Have people been killed/injured?
- Are our staff/customers/other stakeholders accounted for?
- If not, what is being done to achieve that?
- If appropriate, open communications with the emergency services
- What are they doing/saying?
- What help do you require and how can you help them?
- Is there a public health risk?
- Are there technology (IT, telephony) issues and if so what is being done to resolve them?
- Brief summary of issues/risks and what decisions are required to overcome them.

Communication Strategies

Strategy layout

Prepare to communicate

Once the situation has been assessed and if the communication plan is activated a series of tasks will follow:

- Activate call cascade (link to relevant appendix)
- Inform switchboard/receptionists to put all media calls through to the communications room
- Activate incident communications room
- Activate extra phones lines (link to relevant appendix)
- Call-takers in place (see Chapter 10)
- Check who is available and reallocate roles and responsibilities as necessary (see Chapter 5)
- Keep CEO and senior executives informed
- If appropriate prepare to send press liaison officer to site of incident
- Determine which, if any, authorities/regulators need to be informed
- Draft statement for staff and other internal audiences
- Decision on whether/when to issue press release/holding statement
- Draft statement – get sign off for its release
- Check all facts before press statement is released – fast-moving events may mean the situation has changed
- Decision on whether to hold press conference (see Chapter 6)
- Start to prepare 'lines to take' for the media
- Prepare questions and answers (Q&As), outlining probable media questions and appropriate answers
- Brief company spokesperson
- Discuss media strategy – what will we say? How will we say it and when?
- If appropriate continue to liaise with emergency services
- Are their messages consistent with your messages?
- Start media contact record
- Note-taker in place – information time-coded as it arrives
- Activate incident website (see Chapter 11)
- If reporters arrive at your offices make press liaison officer available
- Follow up media enquiries
- Keep media advised of time of future press releases/press conferences, etc.
- Brief or draft statement for other stakeholders as appropriate.

Strategy layout

Media monitoring

- Media monitors in place (see Chapter 9)
- Continually adjust media strategy in light of media coverage
- Correct factual errors if they occur
- Become centre of media focus for release of information
- Provide steady drip-feed of information – if new facts are not available provide colour.

Strategic intent, main effort and the six questions

Crisis Solutions are incident specialists. Over many years they have developed innovative and creative ways of preparing people to deal with emergencies. This is particularly true of strategic intent (SI), main effort (ME) and the six questions (TQ6). To explain: these concepts lie at the heart of Crisis Solutions' thinking on how to prepare and deal with an incident and while they were not originally designed for use in communications, such is their flexibility and proven worth they work as well in PR as anywhere else.

Strategic intent

At the outset of an incident it is important to determine what a successful conclusion to the emergency will look like. This is the SI and is the desired outcome or conclusion. If the incident is a journey then the SI is the arrival at the desired location.

A typical SI might be 'to take such actions in all areas of communication that will protect the staff, business operations and reputation of our organization'. The job of the SI is to provide a unifying purpose for all tactical and operational work. It provides the basis for delegation of authority and flexibility of response.

Once arrived at it becomes the overarching principle that should guide the work of the incident communications room. And one other thing, it is a principle that should not change throughout the duration of the emergency.

Strategy layout

Main effort

Many actions will be required to achieve the SI and a successful resolution. The ME is the priority activity at any given time that must be tackled to help to attain the SI. It should be limited by time and location and unlike the SI may change regularly and often.

A typical ME might be 'we need to assemble the crisis press team'. Once that has been achieved the ME might become 'we need to formulate a Q&A for the CEO'. The ME attracts priority allocation of resources. It should be communicated widely to ensure that the skills and commitment of all concerned are fully employed.

So at the outset of an incident those in charge of the press room must determine the SI and constantly monitor and change the ME to attain the desired conclusion.

The six questions

This is essentially a checklist to aid decision making.

1. What is the impact?
    - What is the scope and nature of the incident?
    - Will the impact get any worse?
    - What information is required and who is best placed to provide it?
2. What are we trying to achieve (the SI)?
3. What needs to be done to achieve the SI?
    - Bear in mind that people must be your priority.
    Thereafter consider:
    - Reputation
    - Performance and service delivery.
4. Which activity has the highest priority now (the ME)?
5. What resources are required to achieve the identified activities?
    - Technology and telephony
    - People
    - Finance
    - Facilities and logistics.
6. What is the best way to co-ordinate the response?

And, finally, though these are described as the six questions there is a sting in the tail and that is the seventh question.

Strategy layout

7. Has the situation changed significantly? If it has, then it is time to go back to the top and re-evaluate the situation and to go through the six questions once again.

These concepts and questions can then be used to formulate a plan to tackle the problem.

Incident management team

In a wider context, an incident management team (IMT) will typically use these concepts. Their tasks may include: information gathering, situation assessment, decision taking, and dissemination of decisions and information.

An agenda for an IMT meeting will look something like this:

- Log or minutes to be kept by note-taker
- Confirm attendance
- Establish detail of incident and asses impact
- Open communication links
- Identify key issues and priorities
- Confirm responsibilities of IMT
- Establish SI and ME
- Determine other priority actions which might involve: HR, security, the media, other areas of the business
- Start to develop 'lines to take' for both internal and external communications
- Draft a status report which may include:
  - injuries to staff (other HR issues)
  - assessment of the incident
  - security at incident site
  - estimate of time to recover
  - legal implications
  - media implications
  - composition of any inquiry team
  - actions to be taken
- Issue instructions to all staff
- Remind staff not to talk to the press
- Consider press release/press conference
- Other possible considerations:
  - cost of recovery
  - long-term implications

Strategy layout

- insurance implications
- health and safety
• Decide time and location of next meeting.

> ## *What have I learned from this chapter?*
>
> - A communication plan should contain a statement of intent
> - An aide-mémoire, at the front of the plan, will help to guide the communications team through the early part of an incident
> - More detailed facts, which might clog up the aide-mémoire, should be readily accessible in the form of appendices
> - An SI and ME are effective tools for overcoming an emergency.

5. How the strategy migrates to a plan

'The problem with communication is the illusion that it has been accomplished.' George Bernard Shaw

The communications team

An incident communications team will:

- Be invoked by an on-call press officer (if the incident happens out of office hours)
- Stay in close proximity to senior management
- Act as the hub for all internal and external communications
- Act as the focus for all journalist enquiries.

A call-out system (see Chapter 11) needs to be in place to enable the communications team to meet without undue delay.

The early hours and days

During the initial phase of an incident it may be necessary to staff the communications room on a 24/7 basis. Careful consideration needs to be given as to how this can be achieved. It is sometimes suggested that staff can work on a 12 hours on/12 hours off basis. Given the enormous pressure generated by an emergency this might well mean your staff are exhausted after 48 hours.

For people to work effectively and think clearly a maximum of eight hours on shift is the most that many can manage particularly if there is to be no break at weekends. Do not forget to allow an overlap when a new shift arrives so people can be brought up to date.

What can you expect?

Incidents come in many forms but a major emergency will generate a huge amount of calls not just from the media but from many other stakeholders too.

A call-taker or press officer might have to answer up to 40 calls in a day. Because of the time involved, press officers actually talking to and briefing the media will

How the strategy migrates to a plan

be involved in far fewer calls and those (the CEO or chief spokesperson) giving set-piece interviews, particularly for television, should limit these to no more than three or four a day.

If press officers are briefing the media make sure, if possible, that they do so at the beginning of their shifts when heads are clear. Press officers will of course develop Q&As and frequently asked questions (FAQs), which will help those responding to telephone questions. These will need to be updated regularly as the incident unfolds.

It is vital there are enough phone lines and enough people to operate the phones as one way to enrage all stakeholders is for them not to be able to get what they will consider to be vital information. Someone must also take responsibility for seeing that the team is fed and watered – food and drink may need to be brought in – and that when an individual's shift finishes that person actually leaves and gets some rest.

In times of emergency some see their roles as indispensible, which may be true, but unless they have eaten and slept they will not be able to operate with their usual acumen and vigour. People cope with stress in many different ways and managers must learn to be tolerant, but food, sleep and exercise are generally recognized as a good starting point.

Roles and responsibilities

The roles and responsibilities of those who make up an incident media press room need to be carefully defined. Typically an incident communications team will be relatively small and nimble, but should be able to make use of other staff to perform duties as required. A communications team might look something like the one outlined in Figure 5.1.

Figure 5.1 – The communications team

How the strategy migrates to a plan

Each of the team members should have significant experience and particular skills that will help them communicate during an emergency. As part of your pre-planning back-up personnel will need to be identified to as it is likely that when an incident strikes some key staff will not be available.

CEO/chief spokesperson

The two may be one and the same or they may not. Typically an entrepreneur who has set up a company will want to be the company's mouthpiece. Unfortunately talking to the media during the course of an incident is very different from announcing the company's results at the AGM or indeed giving an after-dinner speech. Some individuals perform well in a hostile situation, others do not.

The head of communications must make sure whoever is selected to speak for the company during an emergency knows what is expected of them, has been trained and is up to the job. Regular media training is essential for whoever performs this role – a log needs to be kept as to when and how often this occurs (see Chapter 8).

During an incident it is generally desirable for there to be one company spokesperson. Ideally they become the face of the organization that the public begins to know and trust. On a day-to-day basis press officers will continue to brief the media, but for a major interview, particularly on television, this must fall to the chief spokesperson, as will all press conferences.

Head of communications

This individual will likely have several years' experience of working in communications and should be in constant contact with the CEO/spokesperson. The tasks associated with this role will be many and various. They will:

- Develop key messages and 'lines to take' for both internal and external audiences
- Communicate with the media
- Help to prepare and sign off statements released to the media
- Prepare statements for use by the company spokesperson at press conferences
- Oversee the running of press conferences (see Chapter 6)

How the strategy migrates to a plan

- Be at the chief spokesperson's side when they give interviews
- Determine third-party contacts to be used as spokespeople to endorse the company's handling of the incident
- Oversee the running of the communications room:
    - manage a team of press officers
    - ensure media monitors are in place
    - ensure call-takers are in place
    - determine frequency and agenda of daily meetings
- Constantly update CEO and other senior executives on incident status
- Will either be writing or at least overseeing the company's incident communication plan.

As indicated, the head of communications needs to stay in close proximity to the chief spokesperson and this goes for the communications team too. Although in theory it should be possible to brief the spokesperson electronically in an incident it is highly beneficial for the head of communications and indeed other press officers to brief executives face to face. If the spokesperson travels during an incident, the head of communications must accompany them if at all possible.

Under normal circumstances the head of communications may pick up the phone and talk to the media and indeed to other stakeholders. If staffing allows, this should not happen during an incident. The head of communications needs to be the planner who devises a communications response. Picking up the phone, a job that should be done by call-takers or press officers, will only get in the way of the planning process.

Although it falls beyond the remit of this book, business continuity plans are often constructed around a model used by the police of 'gold, silver and bronze'. In simple terms 'gold' are the thinkers, 'silver' are the planners and 'bronze' are the doers or those getting their hands dirty.

For an effective response to an incident it is important that these roles are not confused. Thus when the head of communications picks up the phone only to hear a journalist asking for the location and time of the next press conference that is a waste of their time. Let the thinkers think, the planners plan and the doers do! Easy to write, less easy to achieve.

How the strategy migrates to a plan

Press officers

In most companies there is typically an out-of-hours press officer and as incidents have a nasty habit of making their presence felt at about 3 a.m. on a Saturday it may well be that person who learns of the situation first and has to locate the communications team.

Press officers will:

- Take calls from the media and other stakeholders
- Draft FAQs and Q&As tailored to key audiences for sign off by head of communications
- Draft 'lines to take' and key messages for sign off by head of communications
- Draft holding statements and press releases for sign off by head of communications
- Brief journalists and give phone interviews
- Ensure the smooth running of press conferences and other media events (see Chapter 6).

Internal communications

There is an old joke in PR that goes, 'How many spokespeople does your company have?' To which the answer is, 'Roughly the same amount as there are staff.'

Almost all companies insist that only dedicated specialists speak to the media, but it often does not work out that way. If journalists are not getting what they want from the communications team then they will call every number in the book that relates to your company to find someone who will talk.

This is just one of the reasons why internal communications are as important as external, because what is internal one minute can become external and in the press in the next.

It is often easy to forget about staff during a crisis and deal with stakeholders screaming for information, whether they are journalists, customers or suppliers.

How the strategy migrates to a plan

I know what is going on – but does everyone else?

A common mistake is the assumption that just because a piece of information is well known in the communications room that this is understood elsewhere in the company. Facts and messages must be properly drafted and transmitted to internal audiences. Take a look at what Shaw had to say on the topic at the start of this chapter.

Internal communications are also important because staff morale can go into swift decline if people do not know what is going on, or are left to glean all their knowledge of the situation from the media. Your staff should be the first to know about an incident and they must stay informed.

Internal communications staff will need to draft key messages for internal audiences, with the proviso that anything that is voiced internally will inevitably find its way to the media. On occasions these messages can be quite bland: 'Despite what is going on it is business as usual for our company' or 'When the facts come out the company will be shown to have done the right thing.'

Sometimes there may be very important instructions for staff members to follow to ensure their safety. The internal communications team may also need to draft more detailed information packs for staff consumption. If possible, brief all staff personally, though obviously in a larger or multinational company this will be less feasible. It might also be worth considering a comment box where staff can ask questions anonymously if they are concerned that their questions might seem disloyal.

Above all it is essential that staff are kept up to date and feel they are part of the solution to the incident and not a by-product. Do not allow a lack of information to let the heads drop and morale to dissipate.

Other stakeholders

A communication plan must also include a list, together with contact details, of other stakeholders important to the organization. Press officers will need to make sure their needs are catered for and that statements are drafted and sent to the right audiences, who will include customers and suppliers.

How the strategy migrates to a plan

In some circumstances it may be necessary to hold a meeting to brief key stakeholders. Once again beware that whatever you say to them may well find its way to a reporter (see Chapter 7 for a stakeholder template).

Call-takers

During a major incident the phones are likely to be ringing constantly and you may not have enough staff to take all the calls. If this is the case it may become necessary to draft in members of staff from other departments to take calls.

For them to undertake this work successfully they will need guidance and templates – these can be found in detail in Chapter 10.

Media monitoring

Only through effective media monitoring will you be able to hone your communications strategy and determine whether it is working. Media monitoring is an essential element in incident communications and as such has a chapter all to itself: Chapter 9.

Get everyone involved

As part of the pre-planning stage, when roles have been identified, it is desirable to get those involved to discuss their responsibilities and for them to read a draft of the plan so they can make suggestions as to how it could be improved. A good plan is never set in stone and should be an organic and evolving entity.

And when it's over

In extreme cases, particularly where people have lost their lives as a result of an incident, it may be necessary to offer counselling to your staff. Furthermore, they may have families who will inadvertently have been caught up in the emergency as people bring the company's problems home.

How the strategy migrates to a plan

It may be appropriate to write a letter during or after the incident addressed to family members recognizing their support during a difficult time and the importance of the role played by their family member in overcoming the incident.

The letter might look like this:

Sample letter to families

Dear [insert name],

I would like to offer my thanks to the whole family while [insert name] has been working to help us overcome this most unfortunate incident.

[insert name] has been central to our efforts and has played a significant role in bringing about a successful resolution.

Inevitably work life spills into home life and I want you to know we value the help and support that only families can provide when loved ones are caught up in an [incident/tragedy/emergency] of this nature.

It would be impossible for our company to operate without the help of family members and we appreciate that help enormously.

Yours sincerely,

[Insert name], CEO

Gizmos, gadgets and equipment

The communications room must be properly equipped to handle an incident. This needs to be achieved as part of your pre-incident planning and should include at least some of the following:

- Computers with internet access/group email contacts/stakeholder contacts, including journalists
- Extra phone lines (make sure ahead of time that IT knows what your requirements are likely to be and that they can be accommodated)
- Fax machines (stakeholder numbers should be pre-programmed)
- Whiteboards, calendars and the relevant markers

How the strategy migrates to a plan

- Printers
- Paper
- Envelopes
- Pens
- Photocopiers
- Projector
- Television with access to 24-hour news channels and some recording capability
- Extra mobile phones and chargers
- Media press kits (see Chapter 11)
- Extras tables and chairs
- Paper shredder
- Ability to access and update relevant websites.

Much of the above will be present in most communications rooms. The important thing is to identify additional items likely to be needed during an incident.

What have I learned from this chapter?

- Internal communication is as important as external communication
- Roles and responsibilities within the communications team must be allocated as part of the incident plan
- There should be one chief spokesperson plus a deputy
- The CEO must be in constant contact with head of communications.

6. Press conferences

'In the real world, nothing happens at the right place at the right time. It is the job of journalists and historians to correct that.' Mark Twain

Theatre

There is a theatrical element to press conferences. There is a stage, an audience and a sense of anticipation prior to the event. For those on the podium it can be a pretty high-pressure affair, so like any good theatrical production it must be stage-managed to help those in the spotlight relax and give a convincing performance. For this to happen both the speakers and press officers who run the event will have to understand what is expected of them.

The venue

But before we look at their roles and responsibilities we need to understand what constitutes a good venue.

You may think you have enough space at your head office to hold a press conference and it would have the benefit of the journalists coming to you and your speakers feeling comfortable on their home turf. But are you sure you want journalists at your HQ during the course of an incident? Reporters will inevitably be inquisitive and try to pry, asking questions of other members of staff to get an opinion from the 'shop floor' so to speak.

An alternative may be to look at hotels or conference centres located close to your offices. Part of writing a communication plan will involve finding out the facilities they have to offer and ascertaining costs. But what are you looking for? First of all a venue must have two entrances, one for the journalists and one for those facing the media. You do not want senior executives fighting their way through a pack of reporters to get to the podium.

The room must also be sufficiently large to accommodate journalists commensurate with the nature and scale of the incident that you are enduring – but err on the side of caution and if in doubt go big rather than small.

Press conferences

Memorable example

The Concorde crash happened on 25 July 2000. The plane came down shortly after take-off from Charles de Gaulle Airport at Gonesse, just outside Paris.

It belonged to Air France and had been chartered by a group of German tourists. The British media were searching for a UK angle and found it in the form of Alice Brooking, an attractive Cambridge undergraduate who was working at a hotel that Concorde narrowly missed. Miraculously she escaped with only a few cuts and bruises and gave a press conference at the British Embassy in Paris.

Although this took place two days after the disaster, the crash was still big news, so dozens of journalists turned up. Unfortunately the PR team at the Embassy decided to hold the press conference in a room not much larger than a suburban sitting room – a sitting room that only had one entrance.

The journalists were crammed in like sardines and when Alice arrived she and her Embassy minders had to shove past reporters and cameras – not a relaxed way to face the world's media. Easy access for those giving the press conference is essential – do not forget that as soon as the speaker enters the room the cameras will be turning. Television needs pictures, sometimes called set-up shots, to introduce a personality and their entry into the press conference may be the only pictures available.

So if a spokesperson looks like a rabbit caught in the headlights or has to push through crowds of reporters and their equipment, they are hardly likely to send out the message that they are cool, calm and in control of events.

In days gone by, phones and faxes had to be provided at press conferences, but now most journalists will use their mobile phones and laptops. Security measures must be in place to control the venue, especially if there is a risk of activists attending the event. One method is to have journalists sign in and to check their press credentials. This is not foolproof, however, as pressure groups often employ ex-journalists who take the precaution of keeping their press cards up to date.

Journalists should be issued with a copy of the speaker's opening statement, together with a background information pack. If the statement is time-sensitive,

Communication Strategies

Press conferences

it should carry an embargo time. There is intense rivalry between the print and electronic media and it is wise to keep them apart, if possible.

Ideally there should be a raised platform at the back of the conference hall for television cameras, but this must be robust and stable, otherwise the cameras will not get a steady shot. This has two advantages: it means the cameras, which can be very intimidating, are not too close to the speakers and it allows print and radio journalists to get a clear view of proceedings.

It may be appropriate to use some form of visual prop, such as a company logo located behind the speaker or indeed PowerPoint slides showing pictures or graphs, but make sure these are relevant, clear and add value to the event.

At least one, and possibly many more, press officers will be needed to facilitate the event. Your plan will need a list of possible venues, such as those outlined in Table 6.1.

Table 6.1

Site	Address	Contact	Maximum capacity
[X hotel]	[Street/city/ postcode/country]	[Name/phone number/website address]	[Number of people]
[X hotel]	[Street/city/ postcode/country]	[Name/phone number/website address]	[Number of people]

The role of the spokesperson

There should be one main speaker at a press conference, though it may be appropriate for others with specific technical knowledge to be present. The main speaker, typically the CEO, may not have all the technical data at their fingertips so having someone present who does can alleviate pressure.

Prior to the press conference the main speaker will agree an opening statement with the head of communications or a senior press officer. This is often written by the latter and then altered to suite the speaker's style. It must contain all the

Press conferences

necessary information, but not be overly long, and will be read out prior to questions being taken.

In Chapter 8 we look at how to conduct an interview, and while many of these rules apply to press conferences, suffice to say the main speaker and a senior press officer should prepare for likely questions and responses. During this session key messages that must be transmitted will be agreed and the spokesperson should be pre-interviewed by press officers and asked all the difficult questions. Only by doing this will everyone feel confident about facing the media.

When questions are taken it is essential that the spokesperson listens carefully and replies directly to the journalist that posed the question. It is a mistake to try to take in the whole room with an answer, as the speaker will often appear to lose focus.

Once the press conference is concluded the main speaker should expect extensive one-on-one television interviews. To those not used to this convention it may seem odd to have to face the television cameras individually having just given a press conference, but such is the power of the broadcast media.

From the television journalists' point of view press conferences do not make for very attractive pictures and it always looks more impressive if you are able to conduct a personal interview. Plus television does not like to show their competitors asking the key questions, although it should be mentioned that many 24-hour news channels broadcast press conferences live.

A word of warning: after the press conference there may be many television interviews to undertake if it is a big story, so the spokesperson must ensure that their energy does not flag. The journalists are likely to ask many of the same questions, but the speaker must not appear bored or uninterested because for the journalist and ultimately the viewers this will be the first and probably only time they will be seen.

During the press conference and at subsequent interviews the spokesperson must stay focused and, if possible, keep away from controversial matters that are avoidable. It may require some adroit footwork.

Communication Strategies

Press conferences

> ### *Memorable example*
>
> At the time of the 7 July 2005 London bombings, Brian Paddick was the deputy assistant commissioner of the Metropolitan Police and its chief spokesperson. On the day he gave a press conference together with other members of the other emergency services. Being from the police he received the lion's share of the questions.
>
> All was going well until a reporter from the *Sunday Telegraph* asked why the government's threat level had been reduced to its lowest level since 2001 just a month before the attacks took place. It was like a hand grenade tossed at the podium.
>
> Paddick seemed utterly unprepared for the question. He appeared to justify the decision, which was clearly a decision he had nothing to do with, and it was left to a press officer to help him out and close down this line of questioning by asking journalists to confine their questions to operational matters.
>
> He should not have even attempted to answer such a question, which fell well outside his remit. He could have said, 'I'm not here today to talk about risks or threats – my job is to tell you about the operational response to today's incidents,' and left it at that.

The role of the press officer

Press officers grease the wheels of a press conference – they are central to its smooth running and success. Their first job, once the decision has been taken to hold a press conference, is to alert the media as to when and where it will take place. This can be done through the news wires or simply by phoning or emailing the relevant news organizations.

We have already dealt with the venue, but what about the timing? This may well be determined by events, but 10 a.m. is early enough for the broadcast media to make their lunchtime bulletins. It is also wise to check if any other groups or organizations are holding press conferences at the same time.

If an organization is caught up in what police call a serious incident – perhaps where people have lost their lives – then typically the police will hold a press

Press conferences

conference to which your company may be invited to attend. You must then decide, using your news judgement, whether you wish to take up this offer. If you do then it is essential you talk to the emergency services and determine, as far as possible, what they are going to say. You do not want your CEO to be placed next to a senior police officer who is critical of your CEO or your company. Prior to the event the press office should produce a Q&A identifying all possible questions and suggested responses. This should also contain the key messages that the speaker will need to convey (see Chapter 8). A press officer will prepare an opening statement for the spokesperson and copies must be made available to the media.

When the media arrive, press officers should make themselves available to greet journalists. They should hand out their cards so reporters can call if they have questions when they are writing their story later in the day. Journalists should be invited to sign a register indicating their name, news organization and contact details. Camera operators should be shown where to set up and it should be made clear to television reporters where any one-on-one interviews will take place after the press conference.

When the event gets under way – and it should start promptly at the agreed time – a press officer must introduce the main speakers, setting out clearly who the speakers are, their titles and the correct spelling of their names. They should then make clear how long the press conference will run, which should be no more than an hour (30 to 40 minutes being the optimum depending on the subject). Once the spokesperson has read the opening statement, journalists will then be invited to ask questions. Journalists should be asked to raise their hand if they wish to ask a question and, when called, to state their name and the name of the media organization they represent.

When it is time to wind up the press conference, it is the job of a press officer to announce that there is time for one final question. This takes the heat off the speaker and should reinforce the idea that it is the job of a designated press officer to look after the mechanisms of running a press conference, leaving the speaker to field the questions and not to have to worry about the logistics of the event.

Once the press conference has been successfully concluded a press officer must facilitate the one-on-one television interviews that will take place thereafter. They must agree with journalists the order in which these take place. Given deadlines, this may need sensitive handling. A press officer must be on hand at

Press conferences

all times during these one-on-one interviews to give support and provide factual information should it be required by the interviewee.

If the press conference is to be delayed for any reason then be open and honest with the media. Do not keep them in the dark and give them as much information as you can.

Remember many will have tight deadlines and some may even be broadcasting the press conference live.

Over the internet

Finally, a recent development – especially within the financial community – is to hold press conferences over the internet. Participants are given a website address, username and password and told to log in at a particular time. This has the advantage of journalists being able to take part from their offices.

Currently this only works for print journalists as the pictures are not of sufficient quality for television, but given the pace of change on the internet it is surely only a matter of time before the technology improves and the pictures are used.

Memorable example

Tackling a press conference

Press officers need to keep tight control of press conferences – nothing must be left to chance.

The Frankfurt Stock Exchange was in negotiation to buy its London equivalent. A press conference was called and journalists. Unfortunately, the PR team did not make it sufficiently clear to the television reporters that individual interviews would be conducted after the press conference.

The result was that when it ended a television crew jumped up onto the stage trying to get an interview with one of the speakers – seeing this, all the other crews did the same. With scenes on the stage reminiscent of a rugby scrum, press officers tried to wrest back control and said that following the unruly behaviour of some journalists there would be no further interviews and the event was effectively over. At this point CNN

Press conferences

Business turned up and demanded an interview – unwisely their request was granted only for other television crews to find out and for the rugby match to start all over again.

Journalists are innately competitive. If they see a rival getting an interview or a photo that they were denied they will act with extreme hostility!

What have I learned from this chapter?

- There should be one main speaker at a press conference plus, if appropriate, a technical expert to provide specialist knowledge
- An opening statement, a Q&A and key messages must be prepared prior to the event
- Press officers should pre-interview the main speaker to make sure they are familiar with all likely questions and can respond effectively
- If invited to join a press conference hosted by the police or another organization find out, in advance, what other participants are going to say
- The main speaker will be on camera as soon as they enter the room
- The venue must be of sufficient size and contain one entrance for the press and one for the speakers
- Press officers must take control of the event.

7. Holding statements, press releases and templates

'Words are, of course, the most powerful drug used by mankind.'
Rudyard Kipling

Further plan components

All incident communication plans require a series of templates. If these are correctly prepared and kept up to date they should prove enormously helpful to the communications team in the event of an emergency.

Refer to Chapter 1, which looks at the types of incident to which your company might be vulnerable, and tailor the following templates to suit your needs and your business. They include:

- An initial holding statement
- A grid that incident press releases should follow
- Sample of a more detailed press release
- A key messages template
- Pre-prepared responses template
- Stakeholder template.

Initial holding statement template

Sample holding statement template

Big Trading Company (BTC) press release

Date: [insert date]
Time: [insert time]
Number: [insert number]
Approved by: [insert name]

Holding statements, press releases and templates

> The BTC can confirm that an incident [insert basic details] has occurred at [insert place and time].
>
> Few details are yet available, but our primary concern is for our staff and all those involved in the incident. We are working closely with the emergency services.
>
> The BTC will release further information as it becomes available.
>
> Media enquiries should be made to this number: [insert number].

Typically this and other press releases will be issued to news agencies and all major news organizations – it may also be appropriate to send an amended version to your staff. It is important that all press releases are dated, timed and numbered, making it easy for press officers to establish whether journalists have the most up-to-date information. It is also a useful way of establishing a chronology of events.

Press release grid

As an incident unfolds press releases should follow a grid:

- Time and place of incident
- Details of incident
- Details of casualties (numbers only – names must be released by police)
- An expression of sympathy for all involved if casualties have occurred
- Details of your interaction with the emergency services
- Your wish to embark on a thorough investigation
- Details of impact on environment, if applicable
- Impact on your ability to continue operations
- A quote from the CEO or senior executive
- Time and place of next press conference, if applicable.

Do not forget during an incident that people must remain your priority at all times.

Holding statements, press releases and templates

A more detailed press release

> Sample detailed press release
>
> **Big Trading Company (BTC) press release**
>
> Date: 2 March 2009
> Time: 2.30 p.m.
> Number: 6
> Approved by: Paul James
>
> The BTC can confirm that as a result of the explosion that took place earlier today near Trading House, 12 people he been killed and seven others have been taken to hospital.
>
> The BTC would like to extend its sympathies to all those caught up in this terrible incident: to the families of those who have lost their lives and to those who have been injured.
>
> The CEO, John Salvador, said: 'To many who work at the BTC it is like an extended family and today we have lost members of our family in the most appalling of circumstances; we all feel this loss very deeply.'
>
> We are working closely with the emergency services, who have done a remarkable job in the most difficult of circumstances.
>
> While the care of our staff is our priority, we are endeavouring to continue business and to that end have invoked our business recovery plans, which are enabling us to continue operating.
>
> For more information call the press office on: 07973 2867
>
> The CEO will be holding a press conference at the London Palace Hotel today at 2.30 p.m.

It would perhaps be useful to include a few short bullet points on what should be contained in a successful press release:

Holding statements, press releases and templates

- Prominent company logo – so the recipient can instantly see who it is from
- A press release must immediately make clear what the story is about
- Do not overly complicate the press release – it must be simple and easy to understand
- A press release must answer the journalists' mantra: who, what, when, where and why
- It should, if possible, only be a single page
- Include the name of the person to be contacted and their correct phone number (if the contact is not the person who has written the press release, let them know to expect calls – they must be fully briefed on the story)
- If possible, target a particular journalist with the press release
- Make sure the information is newsworthy – wait until you have something with enough substance before issuing a press release
- Press releases are designed to transmit facts: opinions should be expressed in quotes (clearly state who is being quoted and their relationship with your organization)
- Check every fact contained in the press release and then check again.

Key messages template

For press officers tasked with answering media questions, particularly over the phone, key messages should help to keep them on track, on message and on time.

Key messages template

Key messages (probably around three or four), which may contain some or all of the following:

- Expression of sympathy – people must remain your priority
- Praise for the emergency services and other key responders
- A willingness to resolve the problem and, if appropriate, engage with any enquiry that might follow.

What we know (journalists' mantra):

- Who
- What
- When
- Where

Holding statements, press releases and templates

- Why.

What we do not know:

- If possible, provide an indication as to when certain information may become available and what form it will take (e.g. press release/briefing/interview)
- Commitment to get back to journalist when information is available

Looking ahead:

- Anticipated time of next press release/press conference or interview opportunity
- Time, date and name of staff member who compiled this key message report
- Time and date of next scheduled update.

Pre-prepared responses

For call-takers and press officers the following pre-prepared responses may be useful and can be tailored to your needs:

- 'All I can confirm right now is that an incident occurred at [insert time] at [insert place and give brief details]. Our primary concern is for our staff and all those involved in the incident. We are working closely with the emergency services. We'll get back to you when we know more.'
- 'We've only just heard about this and don't yet have the full facts. Give me your contact details and I'll get back to you.'
- 'Please don't ask me to speculate about the cause of the incident – you would be far better off putting those questions to the emergency services. Right now our priority is to get the situation under control.'
- 'It's far too early to tell. I'm sure you wouldn't want me to mislead you – when we know more we'll get back to you.'
- 'I'm not an expert on that – let me see if I can find someone who is.'
- 'We don't have anything for you right now, but as we speak a statement is being prepared so give me your contact details and I'll make sure it gets to you as soon as it's complete. That should be in the next [insert number] minutes.'

Holding statements, press releases and templates

- 'We need information as much as you do and we are working flat out to establish the facts – please be patient.'
- 'We have plans and procedures in place to deal with situations like this – those plans have been invoked and they are working.'

Stakeholder template

Every organization will have key stakeholders. They may be customers, suppliers, government regulators or competitors. During the course of an incident it is essential to take their temperature and to react swiftly and positively should it be necessary. Although we live in a blame culture and journalists will be demanding to know, 'What caused this?' and 'Who is to blame?' your stakeholders may be far more interested in your ability to cope with and overcome the emergency. The causes and subsequent blame can come later.

Stakeholder template

A stakeholder template might look something like this:

- Name of stakeholder
- Why is this stakeholder important?
- What is likely to be the stakeholder's reaction to the incident?
- What might change this reaction?
- What outcome from this incident would satisfy this stakeholder?
- How can we deliver that in a timely fashion?
- Key messages that we want to convey to the stakeholder.
- Other strategies to win over the stakeholder
- Strategies to get stakeholder involved or alternative strategies to stop the stakeholder from getting involved
- Key contact details
- What third-party advocates could we use to support our case with this stakeholder?

You may, of course, need to write a statement or an open letter to a particular stakeholder. Here is an example that could be employed by a hotel or restaurant where food poisoning has occurred:

Holding statements, press releases and templates

> Sample letter to a stakeholder
>
> Dear Guest (insert name)
>
> We have recently witnessed an outbreak of [insert name of illness] at [insert name of hotel]. It has been determined that after consuming [insert name of dish] at [insert name of hotel restaurant], approximately [insert number of guests] guests became ill.
>
> Those most seriously ill were immediately taken to hospital for treatment. All other guests remained at the hotel, where staff members are looking after them around the clock. We have contained the outbreak and no other guests have reported feeling unwell.
>
> The cause of the [disease/illness] is still to be determined. Meanwhile, the dish that caused this most unfortunate incident has been taken off the menu. We are currently contacting distributors to help us in our investigations.
>
> We are taking all necessary precautions to ensure this does not happen again. Thank you for your understanding and support.
>
> Yours sincerely
>
> Insert name

Templates will also be required for media monitors (see Chapter 9) and for call-takers (see Chapter 10) whether they are trained PR specialists or staff drafted in from other departments.

What have I learned from this chapter?

- Templates form an integral part of an incident communications plan
- Craft pre-prepared press statements applicable to your organization
- Journalists may shout the loudest but other stakeholders must not be forgotten.

8. Coping with the press pack

'Wise men talk because they have something to say; fools, because they have to say something.' Plato

Best practice for dealing with the media

The media can intimidate even seasoned PR staff when it is in full cry. The sheer number of phone calls and relentless media interest can be overwhelming. Being under the media spotlight is a challenge but can provide unique opportunities to disseminate your side of the story to the public.

It is important to maintain good relations with journalists and to be polite and helpful, but ultimately it is their audiences you will want to address. Successful interaction with the media during an emergency requires those in the communications room to think like reporters and devise and concentrate on key messages.

You cannot control what journalists write or say but you can have considerable influence. Above all you have control over what you and or your organization say and do and have the chance to establish your company as a reliable and credible source of information.

Use this checklist to help to achieve these goals:

- Reply to reporters' questions promptly – become their main source of information if you do not you may lose control of the story
- Get the facts – be specific
- Be open and honest
- Help the media to get their job done
- Stay in touch with the public mood
- Show compassion and concern – if people have lost their lives or have been injured you must make an expression of sympathy
- If appropriate, praise the work of the emergency services and what your staff members are doing to resolve the crisis
- The communications team must attempt to co-ordinate the release of information with the emergency services/responding authorities

Coping with the press pack

- If your chief spokesperson contributes to a press conference given by the police try to establish beforehand what the police are going to say
- The chief spokesperson and other senior executives must be thoroughly briefed and constantly updated on the status of the incident (at each briefing there should be a recap of the situation and an indication of what new information is being provided)
- If there is important new information, it should be shared with the media as quickly as possible
- As far as possible be even-handed with the press – do not show favouritism
- It is the job of the police to release the names of staff injured or killed
- Do not give the media access to the families of anyone injured or killed
- Keep a log of reporters who have called the communications room together with their questions and actions taken (see Chapter 10)
- If there is little new information, provide background and colour – supply a steady drip-feed of information
- If journalists sense you are hiding something they will continue to dig
- If they feel that everything has come out, then they are more likely to leave you alone
- Remember the media have many sources other than you – if members of the public are unhappy with the way you have handled something it will be impossible to keep it under wraps
- Pre-empt negative aspects of a story by alerting the media to the actions you are taking to overcome the problem
- Speak with one voice – the media loves to play divide and rule
- Meet a crisis head on and give it the most positive treatment you can
- If you say your organization is doing something, make absolutely certain it really is taking place
- Check all facts before they are released to the media
- Do not speculate – if you cannot answer a question say the matter is under investigation
- Do not be bullied – get back to journalists as soon as you have the facts they require
- Internal communication is not only important for formulating your media policy but also for keeping your staff briefed and aware of how you are coping with the incident
- Leaving staff in the dark undermines morale – brief them before or at the same time as you brief the media
- Staff will be seen as potential interviewees by the media and can start leaks and rumours – make sure they are briefed correctly

Coping with the press pack

- Prepare a biography of those (i.e. the CEO) who will face the press
- Make sure the head of communications is involved in all major decisions taken by senior executives – they will have a good ear as to what will play well with the media and, by extension, the public
- Never lose your temper or use sarcasm with reporters/never walk away from an interview
- Maintain a calm and helpful exterior and avoid appearing overwhelmed
- Beware of laying blame on others
- Use your website – it has the unique ability to inform staff, journalists and the general public simultaneously as to what you are doing to overcome the incident
- If your website does not reflect the emergency it will appear to journalists and the public that you are not in control of events
- People must remain your priority.

Interview techniques for both the written and electronic media

Prior to an interview

Part of the communications team's job will be to outline and agree messages and 'lines to take'. In a normal news interview it is commonly accepted that there will be a minimum of three key messages that must be transmitted no matter what questions are asked. Q&As will have also been written, which should address the hard questions and suggest appropriate answers.

Prior to a major press or television interview all this information needs to be assimilated by the spokesperson who should then be pre-interviewed in an aggressive manner by a press officer to make sure all angles are covered. It will be the job of a press officer to have the following information available:

- The reporter's name and contact details
- What media organization the reporter represents
- Why the reporter wants to conduct the interview
- Who else is being interviewed on the topic
- When and where it will be published or broadcast.

A diligent press officer will also attempt to find out likely questions and reasons why the reporter wishes to conduct the interview – though during an incident the answer to these two questions may be painfully obvious. You can request

Coping with the press pack

that certain questions are not asked/certain topics are not brought up during an interview. Reporters may respect this but it is not likely and they do not like it. Do not be surprised if those questions emerge and be prepared with an answer.

During an interview

From the outset it is up to the person giving an interview to take control of the situation, drive the event and get messages across. Some people imagine an interview is just filling the gaps between the reporter's questions – a far more proactive response is called for.

Do not let the reporter dictate the tone of the interview. If they use very negative words to describe you or your company be careful not to repeat these words in your answers. If a reporter is suggesting your company is run incompetently do not say, 'We are not incompetent'. Simply say, 'That is not true – we understand very clearly what we do and have a clear idea as to how to overcome this incident.'

Listen attentively to the questions – it is amazing how few people do, and be as accurate as you can. Tell the truth, that way you do not have to remember what you said. Never attempt to mislead a journalist – word will spread that you cannot be trusted. It is also a good idea to keep your answers short. This is particularly true during the course of a hostile interview when people sometimes attempt to ramble their way out of questions. If you make a short reply it forces the reporter to ask another question, and the more you say the greater the risk of saying something you wish you had not.

It has been said many times before, but beware of using jargon and acronyms. Chances are the reporter will not understand you and, by extension, neither will your audience. Under normal circumstances, whether in print or broadcast, everything said before, during and after an interview is fair game. Only say to a journalist what you would be proud to say live on the 10 o'clock news. Do not lose your cool, do not be sarcastic and above all do not get up and walk out.

Who holds all the aces?

It can seem in an interview situation that reporters have all the advantages. They know the questions they are going to ask and it is you, not them, that is being

Coping with the press pack

put on the spot. They decide what elements go into the story and will have at least some control over the editing process.

You can ask to see an article or a television news package before it is printed or broadcast, but very few reporters will agree. They may agree to read back direct quotes or facts that have been provided to ensure they are correct.

But you have advantages too. Inevitably you will know more about the story, at least from your perspective, than the reporter ever will. You can influence the location and timing of the interview and above all you decide what messages you want to deliver.

Linking your messages

Messages are the key element to any interview or briefing you give to the media. But these messages will only be of use if they get reported. This is where linking comes in.

The link is a useful device that allows an interviewee to go from answering a question, perhaps even a hostile question, to delivering a key message: respond to a question in a compressed manner and then use a verbal link to take you to a message. For example, 'But surely we are getting away from the real point here which is …' and then link to your message.

Other examples of links:

- 'All of which is true, but I must emphasize that …'
- 'It is important to remember …'
- 'The fact of the matter is …'
- 'That is just not true, the point is …'
- 'I know that is what is being said, but actually …'.

Answer a question and immediately link to a message before the reporter has time to put another question. All this takes some practice and that is where media training comes in. Repetition and consistency of message is important but it must be done in a seemingly natural way – with the proviso that 'natural' in this case means intensive training and preparation.

By consistently linking to your key messages there is a far greater chance of them reaching and being understood by your audience.

Coping with the press pack

Going 'off the record'

An 'off the record' interview should never be entered into lightly. In most instances you are unlikely to feel the need to go 'off the record' with a journalist, but there may be occasions when you want to get information out into the public domain but not have your name or your company's name attached to it.

'Off the record' briefings need to be handled carefully, but the essential rules are: never give such a briefing other than to a journalist you know well and trust, and prior to the event establish exactly what both you and the reporter mean by 'off the record'. There are no formalized definitions but 'off the record' can mean that a journalist can use what you say, but not your name or your company's name as the source. Thus it might read, 'News One has learned that …'. 'Off the record' can also mean that none of the information imparted by you to the reporter can be used in any form.

The purpose of this type of briefing is to bring the reporter up to speed as to where you think the story might be going. Never try to flip between being 'on the record' to being 'off the record' as it will only make for confusion and could have serious consequences.

Media training

The CEO/chief spokesperson and at least three other senior executives must undergo intensive media training with the expectation that they may have to face the press. Press officers may also benefit from refresher courses.

The training must include:

- A general understanding of how the press operates during an incident and what can be expected of them
- Coverage of issues relating to how quickly the media hear about an incident, how the level of media response can vary, what the press are looking for on arrival and what should be said
- Potential incident news scenarios must be used as the basis for interview training
- Live down-the-line television interviews with no reporter present and questions heard through an earpiece
- A series of recorded television and radio interviews

Coping with the press pack

- The ways in which newspaper interviews differ from the electronic media
- An analysis of all interviews and guidance given until tangible improvements are made
- A constantly updated log of who has been trained.

It is important to remember that you cannot be 'media trained' for life. Your spokesperson should have additional training to prepare for specific interviews. Senior executives are routinely busy and often have little time for such training. The head of communications must insist, but keep the training short and sharp.

Preparation is the key to projecting a positive image and conveying your message. This cannot be overstated. Successful interview preparation involves creating a message strategy for each interview and sticking to it.

What have I learned from this chapter?

When talking to journalists:

- Appear willing and eager to give honest answers
- Avoid being defensive, hostile or angry
- Use links to help deliver your messages
- Do not allow the way a question is asked to dictate the response.

9. Media monitoring

'Banality is a symptom of non-communication. Men hide behind their clichés.' Eugene Ionesco

Do we need this?

Larger companies use media monitoring services as a matter of course. It may be expensive, but for marketing and keeping a weather eye on your organization's fortunes it is often deemed essential. If many feel it is essential to know what the media is saying in normal times, it is even more important during an incident.

Only through a careful scrutiny of the media will you be able to respond to its needs and demands. Media monitoring will help you establish whether you are getting your messages across and whether your media strategy is working. It can also help you to identify and then correct any errors that are being reported.

Media monitoring is of particular importance when a spokesperson is about to address the media, given that they must know what is currently in the public domain if they are not to be wrong-footed by a reporter's question. The last thing a company wants is for a journalist to appear to know more about a story than the person giving the interview. Equally, a senior press officer accompanying the spokesperson must be fully briefed for the same reasons.

Media monitoring should also help senior executives in their decision making and inform the strategy employed by the communications team.

In-house monitoring

For the moment let us leave aside those larger companies that can afford to outsource this service. For smaller companies that want to perform the task themselves, it has recently become at once easier and more difficult.

Media monitoring

Taking the latter point first, the huge proliferation of news outlets and the potential for bloggers and so-called citizen journalists to cause mischief has increased exponentially. Put simply there is just so much more news to monitor.

At the heart of this is, of course, the internet, which has paradoxically made the job of in-house media monitoring much easier. Almost every newspaper, magazine or trade journal is published on the internet. Articles often appear on a publication's website long before they reach newsagents. To add to that, many articles published on the internet contain a comments section, which allows you to see how some members of the public are reacting to the story.

You can also sign up to Google and Yahoo! news alerts, which are pretty impressive services that let you know when a new story has been published on a particular subject. You will probably also want to monitor blogs that relate to your company or the incident, along with message boards, related forums and YouTube. It may also be appropriate to keep an eye on social networking sites like Facebook and MySpace. You may also want to use Google blog search, BlogPulse and Technorati to keep you up to date on what is going on in the blogosphere. The great thing about these and the news alerts is that they are free.

One problem with in-house media monitoring, however, is television and, to a lesser extent, radio. Increasingly broadcasters are streaming their output on the internet, but at the time of writing this is intermittent and at best incomplete. Therefore, designated media monitors are going to require access to 24-hour rolling news channels.

Memorable example

The impact of new news technology

Newspapers and TV news channels will always be news driven, but there is no doubt that technology plays a significant role in the way news is captured. The proliferation of inexpensive digital cameras has largely been responsible for the rise in so-called citizen journalism.

A case in point was the death of news vendor Ian Tomlinson during the protests at the G20 summit in London in April 2009.

An initial post-mortem indicated he had suffered a heart attack and had died of natural causes. His death only became controversial a week later

Media monitoring

when the *Guardian* newspaper obtained video footage which appeared to show Tomlinson, who was not a protester, being struck on the leg from behind by a police officer wielding a baton. The same policeman then appears to push Tomlinson to the ground leaving passersby to come to his aid.

The man who shot the footage, a New York businessman, said, 'The primary reason for me coming forward is that it was clear the family were not getting any answers.'

Technology sent the incident to the top of the news agenda. Without the video footage the story would have almost certainly disappeared.

Staying with the G20 summit, where technology itself actually made the news. For the first time, organizations as diverse at the *Daily Telegraph*, the *Guardian* and Sky used Twitter, the social messaging utility, to gather reports.

Reuters news agency hosted a live discussion with Robert Zoellick, the President of the World Bank, in which he answered questions using Twitter.

Members of the public were able to monitor these so-called Tweets by using Twitter Search.

This may be a raw and unfiltered form of news, but as a blogger commented at the time, 'I was following the G20 protests on both TV (BBC & Sky) and Twitter (dedicated Sky & Al Jazeera twitter feeds plus some citizen journalists). I think we've gotten to the point that, as consumers, we'll be picking and choosing which channels of communication work best for which situations. Media houses will have to ensure that their news comes across well across the different channels or may risk losing out.'

The G20 may prove to have been a turning point for Twitter and its role in journalism.

Media monitoring report form

A simple template to aid those involved in all aspects of media monitoring is required.

Media monitoring

- **Source**: Name of media organization
- **Story**: Précis of story
- **Criticism**: Any criticism levelled at your organization
- **Future**: Flag up where story is going/future developments and issues

Figure 9.1 – Media monitoring report form template

So a typical report form might look like this:

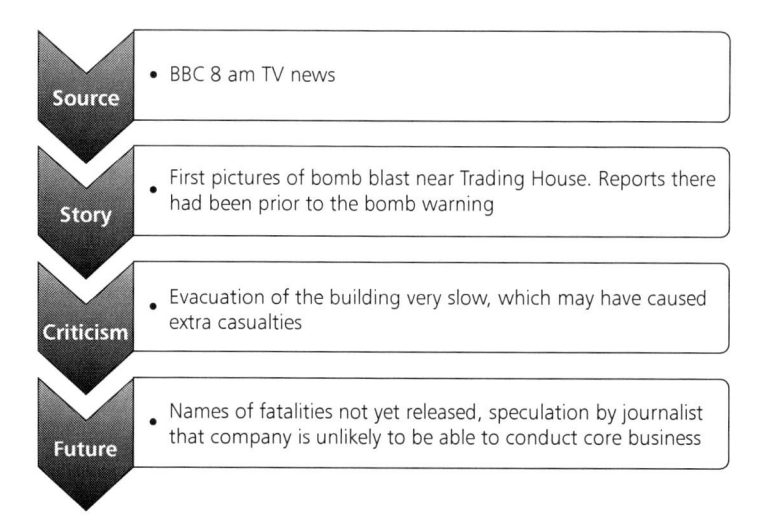

- **Source**: BBC 8 am TV news
- **Story**: First pictures of bomb blast near Trading House. Reports there had been prior to the bomb warning
- **Criticism**: Evacuation of the building very slow, which may have caused extra casualties
- **Future**: Names of fatalities not yet released, speculation by journalist that company is unlikely to be able to conduct core business

Figure 9.2 – Sample media monitoring report form

Media monitoring

Outsourcing media monitoring

A word of caution before we look at outsourcing your media monitoring requirements – even the best media monitoring organizations may not get information to you as quickly as you require during an emergency.

If you have the staff available it is highly desirable that the communications team engage in some form of media monitoring even if all that means is having a 24-hour news channel playing so that when your story makes the news you will know about it straight away.

Some staff should also subscribe to Google and Yahoo! news alerts for the same reason.

When looking to outsource your monitoring there are questions that need answering:

- What media does the service cover?
- Does the service cover all the media outlets that are of interest to you – including speciality or trade magazines?
- Will it add news sources that it does not traditionally cover?
- If you are a multinational company what worldwide news sources will it cover?
- What about foreign language news reports?
- Many online news monitoring services do not sort the wheat from the chaff (if your organization is called by a generic or commonly used word you may receive news that has nothing to do with you – Acme, Orange and Smith come to mind) and the last thing a busy communications team needs is irrelevant clips during an emergency
- Find out how quickly clips can be delivered and in what form
- Some online services only deliver a link to the article and a short extract – what do you require?
- How long do they hold the information?
- How can clips be accessed in the future?
- Accounts are definitely going to want to know what all this costs
- As Americans say, 'look under the hood and kick the tyres' before you sign up.

Do not forget, if you do use a company to monitor the media for you, or indeed if you use a PR firm to help with any aspect of your communications strategy, you need to determine exactly what services you have signed up to.

Media monitoring

By its very nature, an incident is not business as usual. Are you sure your PR firm will be happy working alongside you late into the night? You may have a media monitoring service that delivers clips to you once a day, but will they be willing, at a moment's notice, to up the tempo considerably? These are all questions to be asked in the pre-planning stage so that when one of the communications team calls your PR firm at 6 p.m. you do not discover they have all gone home.

What have I learned from this chapter?

- Only through a careful scrutiny of the media can you respond to its needs and demands
- Media monitoring can help you to identify and correct any errors reported in the press.
- Templates will be required for in-house monitoring
- If you outsource any media services make sure you know exactly what is agreed.

10. Call-takers

'I fear three newspapers more than a hundred thousand bayonets.' Napoleon

Who is calling please?

During a major incident most organizations will struggle to find enough trained press officers to answer media enquiries. It may also not be a valuable use of their time to pick up the phone continually when there are press statements, Q&As and 'lines to take' to be written. One way around this is to get staff from other departments to act as call-takers. The downside is that few will have experience of talking to journalists or to other stakeholders during the high stress of an incident.

Part of your communications planning phase should involve the selection of potential call-takers. If possible they should be given training as to what would be expected of them during an incident. If your company has a call centre, these employees would be ideal candidates as they will have already benefited from training.

Once again templates are called for and it must be made clear to the call-takers that they are not to pass on any information, but merely to fill out the templates. Nevertheless when talking to pushy journalists, irate customers or indeed distraught family members they will need some scripts to follow.

Pre-prepared responses for call-takers

- 'I am afraid I am not able to pass on any facts, but please give me your contact details and your questions and we will get back to you shortly.'
- 'Please do not ask me to speculate about the cause of the incident – I can only take your contact details and questions and I can assure you when we have the information you require we will call you back.'
- 'I am afraid I am unable to answer questions from the media but if you leave your name, your contact details, the name of the media organization you represent and your questions, a press officer will be in touch shortly.'
- 'A press statement is being prepared now, so give me your contact details and I will make sure it gets to you as soon as it is complete.'

Call-takers

Stressful times call for cool heads

During an incident tempers can get frayed. Call-takers are effectively on the front line of an emergency and may have to deal with people who are stressed, hostile, exasperated and upset. Not to mention journalists who do not usually take no for an answer.

Here are some suggestions for dealing effectively with callers:

- Never say 'no comment' to a reporter – it is like a red rag to a bull
- Never hang up on a caller
- However exasperating the caller may be, do not be rude or sarcastic
- Do not tell the person to calm down
- If the caller starts using abusive language, tell them you will not tolerate this by saying 'I am trying hard to help with your problem, but what I will not put up with is verbal abuse' or 'I am trying to help handle your problem, but what I cannot handle is your language'
- Do not be short – allow the caller to talk
- Do not take it personally – you cannot always satisfy the caller
- When interjecting say 'excuse me'
- Appear calm and cool – use a quiet tone of voice and be patient
- Do not say 'you are wrong', 'you do not understand', 'I cannot help you right now', 'things could be worse' or 'that is a stupid thing to say'.

Templates

What follows is a series of templates that will help call-takers to get their job done. All templates can be adapted to suit individual organizations. First, a simple media template is shown in Table 10.1. A more complex media template follows in Table 10.2. A general telephone enquiry template is provided in Table 10.3.

Call-takers

Table 10.1

Media organization	Name and contact details	Date and time of call	Questions	Deadline	Actions taken
Daily Express	Ross Simmons 07775 231 231	2 July 2009 11.35 a.m.	When and where is the next press conference?	ASAP	Journalist told press conference at Hilton Hotel – 2pm today
BBC News at Ten	Stella Smith s.smith@bbc.co.uk 0044 7234 2345	2 July 2009 11.40 a.m.	Requests interview with CEO	6 p.m.	Journalist informed CEO not available today

Call-takers

Table 10.2

Caller's name	
Date and time of call	
Media organization	
Contact details: • Phone • Fax • Email.	
Questions	
Requests: • Interview • Talk with press officer • Press statement • Details of next press conference • Fact check • Other.	
Actions to be taken	
Priority: 1. Immediate response 2. Respond by [insert time] 3. No immediate response necessary.	
Call-taker's name	
Call-taker's phone number/extension	

Communication Strategies

Call-takers

Table 10.3

Caller's name	
Date and time of call	
Media organization	
Contact details: • Phone • Fax • Email.	
Priority: 1. Immediate response 2. Respond by [insert time] 3. No immediate response necessary.	
Nature of call: • Questions • Requests • Complaints.	
Outcome of call	
Actions to be taken	
Call-taker's name	
Call-taker's phone number/extension	

Getting the information to the right people

Once the calls start coming in and the templates are filled, there needs to be a mechanism for getting the information to the right place.

It may well be possible to email the templates to a press officer who is responsible for delegating responsibility for the questions and requests that the calls generate. If call-takers are filling in the forms by hand then some form of collection and delivery will be necessary. This task will need to be assessed and responsibilities delegated as part of the planning process.

What callers hate

The communications planning process must involve anticipating potential problems and finding ways to overcome them. During an incident callers may become frustrated in their efforts to get information from your company.

This is what callers hate most:

- Phone not answered promptly – especially when someone must be there
- Encountering an incompetent telephonist
- Left hanging on without an explanation of what is happening
- Not understanding how the call-taker can help
- The call-taker jumping to conclusions about the caller's needs before the caller has a chance to explain their requirements
- Being forced to answer a series of closed questions that stop the caller from expressing their real needs
- The call-taker ringing off leaving the situation vague, and the caller uncertain about what will happen next
- Being greeted by an answering machine instead of a real person and being given 15 caller options
- Caller being told someone will get back to them – never to hear from the organization again.

> ### *What have I learned from this chapter?*
> - The high level of calls received during an incident may mean call-takers will be required
> - They should be selected as part of the planning process and receive training
> - A series of templates will need to be written to support them.

11. Information, fact sheets and general know-how

'Regardless of how you feel inside, always try to look like a winner. Even if you are behind, a sustained look of control and confidence can give you a mental edge that results in victory.' Arthur Ashe

A grab bag of ideas

Welcome to Chapter 11 which is something of a catch-all for vital pieces of information that need to be contained in your plan, but do not quite warrant a chapter to themselves.

Here we look at call-out and call-cascade systems, details of past crises, press kits, details of your recovery site (if you have one) and perhaps most exciting of all, the contents of the 'battle box'.

Key contacts

If you cannot assemble your team you cannot begin to overcome an emergency. To that end someone has to be tasked with collating and keeping current all contact details of your people within the communications team, as well as wider contacts throughout your organization and beyond.

Contact details for key people must include mobile, home and pager numbers, and email addresses. Be sure to have names spelled correctly together with correct titles. If necessary, have phonetic pronunciation of names to hand in case television and radio reporters are unsure of how to pronounce these.

Call cascade

In a larger company it may well be necessary to implement some form of call-cascade system to assemble your troops. You may wish to consider a computerized system that calls a pre-determined set of numbers with a simple message or employs a system based on short message service (SMS) messaging.

Information, fact sheets and general know-how

These tasks can of course be outsourced as many companies provide such services. However, bear in mind that computers and phones may crash during an emergency so a readily accessible list of contacts (probably in hard copy form) must be available to everyone within the communications team and elsewhere. During out-of-office hours it is essential that an on-duty press officer has easy access to all of this information.

Stakeholder contacts

Another key part of any communication plan is to have contact details for all other important stakeholders. These will include customers, suppliers, the media, emergency services and hospitals. Names and especially mobile phone numbers and email addresses are extremely important. Needless to say someone is going to have to keep this information current as otherwise it will be worthless.

Press kits

If you work in communications you probably deal with reporters on a regular basis. The difference during an emergency is that in all likelihood you will not know the reporters calling and similarly they will know little of your business.

A great deal of valuable time will be lost if you keep answering the same questions asked by different reporters who just need to know the basic facts about your business, such as what you manufacture, the location of your head office, how many staff the company employs, etc. You may already have a press kit that fits the bill but if not it should include:

- Address of the organization's HQ and other relevant sites
- Name and title of the CEO
- Name and title of other executives
- Name of the head of communications and contact details
- Date organization was founded
- Products manufactured/services provided /description of what you do
- Main clients/suppliers
- Number of employees
- Brief company history
- Pictures (contained on a CD) of the CEO, executives, products, HQ and other plants/offices, etc.

Information, fact sheets and general know-how

Incident website

During an emergency your organization's website must reflect the fact that an incident is taking place, you are aware of it and are using your best efforts to overcome it. Too often companies leave their website exactly as it would be in normal times, which frankly can look bizarre. For example, if a travel company is experiencing problems and its website is still extolling the virtues of its holidays it may well look as though the company has not grasped the seriousness of the situation.

It should also be borne in mind that advertising may need to be pulled if it seems out of keeping with the incident that is taking place. As part of your pre-planning you may wish to consider the use of an incident or dark website that is only activated in an emergency. Alternatively, you may just wish to use your regular website to keep customers, journalists and other stakeholders informed. If you do opt for an incident website, remember your normal company website must reflect the fact that an incident is taking place.

A dark website should contain all press releases and company statements that pertain to the incident as well as the information contained in the press kits mentioned above. It thus becomes a useful one-stop shop that journalists covering the story can be directed to, along with other members of the public who want the latest information.

Its other advantage is that it forms a discrete barrier between your normal website and the incident taking place. Rapid updating of your websites will be essential during an incident so, if possible, a member of the communications team should have the technical ability to perform this task.

Fact sheets

For larger companies, particularly multinationals, it is a good idea to have a series of fact sheets that detail all of your offices, factories and plants, including those overseas. If an incident occurs in your Hong Kong office you will need to know who the general manger is and who is in charge of communications – in fact a whole host of information that may not be so easy to come by in an emergency.

Information, fact sheets and general know-how

A fact sheet should contain at least some of the following:

- Name, address and telephone numbers of offices
- Name of the general manager (including photo) and contact details
- Has the general manager received media training?
- If not who can speak to the press?
- Name of communications and HR people including contact numbers
- Brief outline of what the office does/manufactures
- Relevant photographs.

These fact sheets may be similar to the press kits mentioned above but may well contain sensitive information that should not fall into the media's hands.

Recovery site

Many organizations either own or rent a recovery site to which the company can decamp during an emergency. This may appear to be an expensive contingency but can of course pay dividends. It is not the function of this book to dictate whether your organization should have a recovery site, but if you do have one it needs to be properly equipped, easily accessible at any time of the day or night and you will need to know what you will find when you get there.

A fact sheet must be prepared and placed in one of your plan's annexes. It might look like this:

Sample recovery site fact sheet

Recovery Site:
20 Southwark Street
London SE1 0RS

Contact:
Jeff Jones
Regional Workplace Environment Manager
Work: 020 7443 34231
Mobile: 07671 964580

Access to the building during out-of-office hours can be gained via the centre security office. This is located opposite the two towers in the central square at first floor level.

Communication Strategies

Information, fact sheets and general know-how

> Shutters or gates between midnight and 6 a.m. now secure the whole site. Telephone number for the centre is 020 8567 3453 which is covered 24/7.
>
> Video conferencing is available.
>
> The training room is ideal for the communications room and contains five desks with internet-linked computers. It is approx 15m × 6m. It has four direct dial phone lines.
>
> The conference room is of a similar size to the training room and would be suitable for the CEO and other executives. There are no computers *in situ*, but there are IT points so computers can be brought in. There are three direct dial phone lines.
>
> Interview room 1 has two direct dial phone lines.
>
> Each of the remaining interview rooms has one direct dial extension.
>
> There are in total seven small interview rooms.
>
> There are two televisions on site, both with Freeview and video cassette recorder.
>
> There are kitchen and shower facilities.

Whether or not you have a recovery site, and what is contained therein, will be part of your organization's business recovery plan (BCP). Your communication plan will need to include the above details and any others that concern communications-related matters.

Past incidents and emergencies

It is worthwhile keeping a record of any past emergencies that the organization has had to endure as journalists have a habit of connecting past incidents to those of the present day. They may or may not be connected but it is wise to know what has gone before.

This is particularly true of events that happened a few years previously. People move on, organizations change at a rapid pace and those that dealt with a

Information, fact sheets and general know-how

previous emergency may be long gone. What remains is a hazy memory of something bad happening a few years ago. It is likely that this information is held somewhere within the organization, but it may not be readily available and may not be in a particularly user-friendly form.

To that end another fact sheet is required that itemizes the key elements of all past emergencies – keep them brief and to the point. It should contain:

- A brief outline of the incident – what were the particular issues, how did the media cover the story and how did the organization emerge from the event
- 'Lines to take' and messages the organization used to overcome the incident
- Names of key spokespeople (are they still with the company?)
- Any positive case studies that arose from the incident
- Name of any third-party experts employed to speak on the company's behalf
- Name of the individual within the organization who knows most about the incident
- Where to go to seek further information on the incident.

Memorable example

Foot and mouth – lessons from history[3]

In 2001 the UK suffered a massive outbreak of foot and mouth disease, which severely damaged rural economies and played havoc with the tourist trade. The lingering image of the incident for most people will likely be the giant pyres used to dispose of animals killed in the mass cull.

At the time Nick Brown, Agriculture Minister, said, 'I am absolutely determined to do everything possible to extinguish the disease.' One thing he and his department, the Ministry of Agriculture, Fisheries and Food (MAFF), failed to do was to look back to a previous outbreak in 1967. Following that incident the Northumberland Committee produced a report in 1969 that favoured burying rather than burning carcasses. Burying was thought to be quicker than cremation and the report also recognized the danger of thermal currents transmitting the disease and said this was 'further argument for burying in preference to burning'.

In 2001 the Environment Agency saw burial as the least desirable option, primarily because of health concerns over seepage into water supplies. The

Information, fact sheets and general know-how

> preferred option of burning was made extremely difficult because of lack of capacity and became, very quickly, a PR nightmare.
>
> The *Northumberland Report* also recommended early use of the Army:
>
> > *In future it should not be necessary to wait until an outbreak is widespread before obtaining the assistance of military personnel. Circumstances could arise making it highly desirable to call on the Army for some forms of assistance to control the disease even during the course of a single outbreak or a small number of outbreaks; speed and efficiency in slaughter of infected and in-contact animals, disposal of carcasses and disinfection of premises are the most vital elements in controlling an outbreak and these will not be achieved without disciplined workers under experienced and trained supervisors.*
>
> In the early days of the 2001 outbreak MAFF took a 'we are in control' attitude, but soon became overwhelmed. The Army was only brought in a month after the first outbreak when MAFF were removed as lead authority.
>
> In their 2002 report *Bureaucratic Failure and the UK's Lack of Preparedness for Foot and Mouth Disease*, authors Allan McConnell and Alastair Stark say the *Northumberland Report* and a report by the then chief veterinary officer, John Reid, into the origins of the 1967 outbreak were ignored and 'did little more than gather dust'.
>
> A fact sheet highlighting recommendations from these reports contained within the government department's crisis management plan might have helped enormously and persuaded the authorities that cremation was not such a good idea.

Battle box

During an incident a 'battle box' containing emergency supplies, kept in the communications room, could prove very useful. It should be portable, allowing for it to be taken to a recovery site.

The box might contain the following:

- A copy of the plan including all call-out contact details
- Stationery equipment (pens, pencils, paper, stapler, etc.)

Information, fact sheets and general know-how

- Torches/batteries
- Whiteboard/marker pens
- Laptop computer
- Satellite phone
- Mobile phones plus chargers
- Medical kit
- Spare clothing
- Stills camera/video camera
- Tea/coffee/kettle.

In theory this is a good idea; in practice it may prove difficult to contain the supplies as when someone loses their mobile phone or needs a torch they will inevitably dip into the box. Battle box security will need to be enforced.

> ## *What have I learned from this chapter?*
>
> A communication plan should include:
>
> - Current contact details of all key stakeholders
> - Some form of call-out system
> - Press kits
> - Company fact sheets
> - Details of past incidents.

12. Post-incident evaluation

'If you don't read the newspaper, you are uninformed. If you do read the newspaper, you are misinformed.' Anon.

Now can we forget about that?

Once an incident is over it is tempting for all concerned to put it behind them. Emergencies are inevitably traumatic and the instinct to move on is understandable, but one good side to an emergency is that it can provide an opportunity to learn and improve an organization's incident capability.

Following an emergency, an evaluation exercise should be carried out to measure the effectiveness of the communications team and the communication plan. In particular the following elements should be evaluated:

- Response time
- Media coverage
- Staff perception – were staff satisfied with the information they received, what can be improved, etc.

And in more detail:

- Was the incident handled quickly and effectively? If not why not?
- What were your messages?
- Did you get your messages across effectively?
- How did your messages play out?
- Were they reported in the media?
- Were there any miscommunicated messages?
- Did you miss any audiences or people?
- How well did the press room work?
- What could be improved?
- Were more people needed? Fewer people?
- Did you use the communication plan? Did it work? How could it be improved?
- Were the procedures and processes for responding to media enquiries effective?
- Was media monitoring effective?

Post-incident evaluation

- Did call-takers prove effective?
- Were procedures and processes for responding to media requests for interviews effective?
- Were procedures for preparing the CEO/chief spokesperson to talk to the media effective?
- Were procedures for preparing and running a press conference effective?

Stakeholders – how do they feel about your organization now?

What is the public's/media's perception of your organization now? How is it different from before the crisis? Here are some thoughts on how to address this issue – in general, do stakeholders believe:

- All reasonable steps were taken to avoid the incident?
- The company kept in touch with the public mood?
- The organization communicated in a timely, consistent and helpful manner?
- The organization was capable of resolving the issues that emerged?

Within a communication plan someone must be identified and tasked with collecting post-incident data. All those involved – staff and external stakeholders – should be approached for information, including reporters who covered the story. They are likely to be journalists who you know and trust and probably deal with on a regular basis.

Accessing this information can prove tricky and once again templates are called for. Ideally these templates need to be short and specifically targeted at stakeholder groups so that individuals do not have to wade through endless questions that do not relate to them. These questionnaires can be emailed or handed out but in reality results are more likely to accrue if the data collection process is done by individuals over the phone or in person. Those carrying out these interviews should make it clear that the process will take no more than a few minutes, thus encouraging people to participate.

Post-incident evaluation

A template for communications team members might look something like this:

Table 12.1

Name and contact details	
Your role during the incident	
Was the incident handled effectively?	
What is your view of the outcome?	
How well did the press room work? What could be improved?	
Did you use the communication plan? Did it work? How could it be improved?	
How well did communications team members interact?	
Were more people needed? Fewer people?	
Were the procedures and processes for responding to media enquiries effective?	
Did call-takers prove effective?	
Was media monitoring effective?	
Were procedures and processes for responding to media requests for interviews effective?	
Were procedures for preparing CEO/chief spokesperson to talk to the media effective?	
Were procedures for preparing and running a press conference effective?	

Post-incident evaluation

Were the procedures and processes for communicating with staff and relatives effective? If not give reasons and suggestions for improvement.	
Did staff receive regular and accurate communications?	
Was more equipment required? Phone lines? Computers? Television? Fax? Mobile phones? Other?	
Other comments	

A template for other stakeholders might look something like this:

Table 12.2

In your view did the company deal with the incident effectively?	
What went well? What could have been improved?	
Do you view the company differently following the incident? More favourably? Less favourably? Give reasons.	
Did the company communicate in a timely manner?	
Were the company's messages consistent?	
Were the messages helpful?	
Other comments	

Post-incident evaluation

Once these templates have been completed they will provide your organization with a wealth of information that will allow you to update your communication plan and enable you to tackle any future incidents with greater confidence.

A report will need to be written that comes complete with an executive summary and action points. This may well include a plan update, further media training, and a shift in roles and responsibilities. Some of the templates contained within the plan may also need to be rewritten.

An action plan might look like Table 12.3.

A word of warning: the report should not be an attempt to apportion blame or settle scores if some things did not go well during the incident. The purpose of the report is to promote learning and to improve your organization's resilience.

As we saw in the previous chapter, it is important to collate fact sheets giving details of previous incidents – once again these templates will help in that process.

Post-incident evaluation

Table 12.3

Item	Issue	Requirement	Recommended action	Owner
1	The communications team's approach to incident management needs to be documented.	Develop and agree an opening agenda and situation review format.	1. Confirm requirement 2. Agree content and format 3. Document within the current plan.	Head of communications to oversee
2	CEO not comfortable giving television interviews during incident.	Media training.	1. Confirm interview aspects that need to be addressed 2. Determine whether there is in-house capability to deliver training 3. If not appoint outside contractor.	Head of comms to provide media training for CEO
3	The recording of critical information, decisions and actions needs to be formalized.	Establish procedures for recording of key information, decisions and actions. Establish the facility to display the recorded data.	1. Cnfirm the format required, and how it can best be presented 2. Document the procedures and processes 3. Train support personnel.	James Johnson (press officer) has volunteered to draft procedure and update plan

Communication Strategies 83

Post-incident evaluation

> ## *What have I learned from this chapter?*
>
> - An incident can provide excellent learning and increase an organization's resilience
> - Templates are the best way to retrieve information about an incident
> - Specific templates should be written for specific stakeholders
> - Once the information is collated, a report containing an action plan must be produced.

13. Testing the plan

'Freedom of the press in Britain is freedom to print such of the proprietor's prejudices as the advertisers won't object to.' Helen Swaffer

So does the plan work?

Once a plan is written it needs to be tested. This can be achieved in the grip of a real incident or in the more benign form of a plan test. Given that most people would prefer the latter, this chapter sets out the type of plan tests that are available. For further information on plan testing and all aspects of incident simulations please refer to *Exercising for Excellence* by Crisis Solutions, also published by BSI.

An exercise should enable everyone to understand an organization's current incident communications capability. It should highlight areas of a strategy that are incomplete or need changing and can be the strongest argument for additional top–down engagement and resources.

If your plan is in good shape an exercise will instil confidence throughout your organization that you are well placed to survive and thrive in the event of a crisis.

Types of exercises

All exercises are bespoke in that they are tailored for specific participants for specific reasons. The benefit of categorizing exercises is that it gives planners an immediate idea of scale, complexity and planning effort required for different types of events.

To this end, *BS 25999-1:2006* gives a table of 'Types and methods of exercising BCM strategies', which is reproduced in Table 13.1.

Testing the plan

Table 13.1

Complexity	Exercise	Process	Variants	Good practice frequency
Simple	Desk check	Review/amendment of content	Update/validation	At least annually
		Challenge content of BCP	Audit/verification	Annually
Medium	Walk-through of plan	Challenge content of BCP	Include interaction and validate participants' roles	Annually
	Simulation	Use 'artificial' situation to validate that the BCP(s) contains both necessary and sufficient information to enable a successful recovery	Incorporate associated plans	Annually or twice yearly
	Exercise critical activities	Invocation in a controlled situation that does not jeopardize business as usual operation	Defined operations from alternative site for a fixed time	Annually or less
Complex	Exercise full BCP, including incident management	Building-/campus-/exclusion zone-wide exercise		Annually or less

Testing the plan

These definitions provide a broad outline as to the types of exercise available. Regardless of the category, the importance of an exercise is that it achieves its defined objectives.

Simple exercises

A simple exercise is often called a 'desktop' or 'workshop'. It typically involves a small number of people, perhaps 5–20. However, the beauty of a simple exercise is that it can easily accommodate complete teams from various areas of your business. The numbers may increase and with it the logistics but the objectives will remain the same.

A simple exercise will seldom involve the provision of a virtual-world environment or the need for more than everyday resources. Typically, participants will be given a simple scenario and then be invited to discuss specific aspects of a company's plan. It will probably last no more than three hours and is often split into two or three sessions, each concentrating on a different theme. In this case, either two or three different scenarios can be used or one scenario can be progressively developed to introduce themes that need to be addressed.

Real-time pressure is not usually an element of simple exercises. Questions will need to be written ahead of time so that facilitators ensure discussions are productive and germane to the objectives of the event. How long will it take to plan? Just because it is a simple exercise does not mean that the planning and preparation can be less thorough. However, in most cases the planning effort will be in the region of days rather than weeks.

Medium exercises

A medium exercise will invariably be conducted within a virtual world and will usually bring together several departments or teams. The scope of a medium exercise can range from a small number of teams from one organization being co-located in one building to multiple teams operating from dispersed locations.

Attempts should be made to create as believable an environment as possible and the numbers of participants should reflect a realistic situation. Depending on the degree of realism required it may be necessary to produce simulated news broadcasts, together with simulated websites. A medium exercise will normally last between two and three hours – although it can take place over

Testing the plan

several days – and typically involves a scenario cell who feed in pre-scripted injections throughout the exercise to give information and prompt actions.

The total planning effort will depend largely on the complexity of the scenario and the number of different aspects of the plan being addressed. For small-scale exercises, a total of 10 working days spread over two to three months might be sufficient. However, with large-scale exercises 20–30 working days might be required over a six-month period.

Complex exercises

A complex exercise is perhaps the hardest to define as it aims to have as few boundaries as possible. It will probably incorporate all the aspects of a medium exercise and many more. Elements of the exercise will inevitably have to remain within a virtual world, but every attempt should be made to achieve realism. This might include a no-notice activation, actual evacuation and invocation of a recovery site.

While a start and cut-off time will have to be agreed, the actual duration of the exercise might be unknown if events are allowed to run their course in real time. If it takes two hours to get to the recovery site instead of the expected 45 minutes, the exercise must be flexible enough to cater for this. If a key player is unavailable, a deputy must be prepared to step in.

The planning effort required for a complex exercise could conceivably be less than that for a medium exercise if the approach adopted is one of 'this event has happened – stand back and see what happens'. However, in most cases the planning effort will be at the upper end of that for a medium exercise – that is, at least 20–30 working days over a period of up to six months.

Aims and objectives

The overriding consideration must be the exercise's aims and objectives. Why are you doing this exercise and what do you expect to get out of it?

Until you have defined, unequivocally, these aims and objectives there is no point in going any further in the planning process. They are not just a woolly statement at the beginning of the exercise specification; they define for everyone exactly why they are doing the exercise and will drive every action

Testing the plan

thereafter. It will require careful thought and, ideally, endorsement at the highest level.

Who do you want to involve?

The type of exercise you choose will usually dictate who will be involved as participants. As a general rule, the more complex the exercise the more people will be involved. The aims and objectives could also dictate who should participate. Proposed players may demand the inclusion, or exclusion, of specific teams or departments.

Do not make an exercise overly complicated by involving people who are not required just to make the exercise seem bigger. While the intention might be to conduct a medium exercise, if the objectives can be met by conducting a simple exercise with fewer participants then do so. If, however, the exercise objectives can only be met by involving a large number of people from all departments, it will be incumbent on the planners to ensure that the exercise engages all participants sufficiently so that they feel their participation is worthwhile.

Another factor to consider is the availability of the intended participants. With the possible exception of 'no notice' elements of a complex exercise, business as usual activities should not normally be adversely affected by exercises. It is therefore important that the availability of key players and teams is confirmed before detailed planning commences. In this respect it is useful to have high-level management buy in for the exercise programme as this should help resolve any 'availability' issues.

In medium and complex exercises, external stakeholders may be involved, including the emergency services, recovery sites, PR organizations, etc. Ensuring their availability will be essential because without them it could be necessary to scale down the exercise as some objectives might be unachievable. Obviously the same applies if an external specialist is essential to the delivery of a simple exercise.

Planners

Exercises do not plan themselves. When choosing the type of exercise it is essential to ensure that there are sufficient people available to conduct the thorough planning it will involve. Everyone has a 'day job' and so being part of an exercise

Testing the plan

planning team is likely to be above and beyond what they normally do. It is essential that members of a planning team understand exactly what will be required of them and if they cannot guarantee to deliver, they should not be part of the team.

Simple exercises might only involve one or two planners but as the complexity increases, so will the size of the planning team. In more complex exercises that involve external stakeholders, they should be involved in the planning process and might be vital to the success of the exercise. If they cannot commit to the planning requirement it may be necessary to scale back the scope of the exercise. If in-house resources are clearly insufficient, consideration should be given to engaging the services of an external specialist provider.

Case study

Testing the communications team

The background

As part of its ongoing plan-testing strategy, a major European bank wanted to evaluate the incident communication capabilities of both their internal and external communications teams and to allow participants to practise roles and responsibilities in an incident press room.

One of the major challenges when planning the simulation was the number of people involved: 50 members of communication departments from across Europe had to be tested, stretched, kept involved and entertained.

The planning

It was decided that two plausible and challenging news scenarios were required together with a series of injections for each scenario to maintain pressure on the participants. A full-blown master events list was not deemed necessary.

The players were divided into three teams, and each team was then subdivided into two groups. In each team one group played the role of the incident communications room – dealing with both internal and external communications. The other group played the role of journalists, members of staff and members of the public phoning in to the communications room for information. Each group contained approximately eight people.

Testing the plan

Communication between the groups took place using mobile phones. Telephone directories were produced and issued just prior to the start of the exercise. Each scenario lasted about 45 minutes. When the first was completed the groups swapped roles and moved on to scenario two. At the end of each scenario those in the communications room had to produce a press release and a short summary of the messages that the company felt appropriate for release to the media. Those involved in internal communication were tasked with producing a quick initial holding statement for company staff plus a later, more extended version.

To really test the incident readiness of the teams once both scenarios were complete each team had to nominate a spokesperson to face a television interview. A professional journalist and cameraperson were employed to put them through their paces. They were asked questions based on the scenario in play while they were in the incident communications room.

The delivery

These are the two scenarios that were used:

Scenario 1. 'Heartless' bank killed my son

The Euro-Wide Bank (EWB) stands accused today of being partially responsible for the death of 37-year-old Jeremy Dobbs. His mother, Angela Dobbs, broke down as she described how her son, a multiple sclerosis sufferer who lived on benefits, had taken his own life.

Though very ill and entirely dependent on benefits, EWB lent Dobbs £20,000 which he could never pay back. His mother believes the bank's actions directly contributed to his suicide. The five-year loan, swallowing more than half his monthly benefits, came with costly protection insurance. In view of Dobbs's long illness and his inability to hold down a job, it was not worth the paper it was written on.

EWB said, 'The loan was granted based on the information that was provided by Mr Dobbs's credit scoring and the conduct of his bank account.' It added: 'EWB has strict lending criteria. It is not in our interest or our customers' interest to lend money that cannot be repaid.'

Testing the plan

> Yet consumer groups are horrified by the fact that Dobbs was granted such a big loan by a high street bank, even though he was living on benefits. 'It's disgraceful,' says Joe Solomon, chief executive of the Independent Banking Advisory Service. 'This is the most irresponsible piece of lending I've ever come across, they should be ashamed of themselves.'
>
> Solomon says the government must now urgently rein in the excesses of the banks. 'Irresponsible lending is a major issue that the government must tackle head on,' he says.
>
> While looking at pictures of her son in happier times Dobbs's mother said: 'I could see him getting more and more depressed – the money seemed to bear down on him – he knew he could never pay it back and felt he was a burden on us. This is the bank that last year made £10 billion in profits. They seem happy to take the money – now they've taken a life.'

To keep the scenario moving, the following injections or incidents were handed to those asking the questions during the course of exercise play:

Scenario 1, Injection 1

A woman in a wheelchair, Mary Jacobson, has been pushed into the EWB branch at 200 Tranter Street, Birmingham, where she has spoken to staff.

She says she has read the newspapers concerning Jeremy Dobbs and is claiming to be in a similar circumstance.

She is disabled, unable to work, lives on benefits and she too has been lent a substantial sum by EWB (£9,000) which she now says she has no chance of repaying.

She claims that she previously made an offer to EWB to pay off the loan at £20 a month, but this was rejected. Currently the loan is costing her over £200 a month.

She is clearly distressed and is demanding help from EWB staff. If help is not forthcoming she says she will go to the press with her story.

******

Testing the plan

> Players will simulate staff at the Birmingham branch phoning in for guidance.
>
> A few minutes later this story leaks to the media.

> ### Scenario 1, Injection 2
>
> A producer from the BBC Radio 4 World at One programme calls the EWB press office.
>
> Joe Solomon, chief executive of the Independent Banking Advisory Service, has agreed to appear on the show to discuss the Dobbs case and wider issues concerning the lending policy of high street banks. He is expected to be critical of EWB.
>
> EWB is invited to field someone to put their case.
>
> ******
>
> Injection to be handed to a 'journalist' who will assume the role of the World at One producer – a forthright individual who will not let EWB off the hook and points out if a spokesperson does not appear it will look very bad for the organization.

Those phoning into the incident communications room were also furnished with some suggestions as to questions they might ask:

> ### Media
>
> Lines that reporters might be taking:
>
> - Why did EWB lend the money in the first place?
> - What does EWB feel about the man taking his life?
> - Will there be compensation for his mother?
> - What checks will be put in place so this does not happen again?
> - Response to Joe Solomon's comments?
> - Why does EWB sell costly protection on a loan that could not be repaid?
> - Push for press statement/interview.

Communication Strategies

Testing the plan

EWB staff

Questions from staff:

- Is there any truth to the allegations in the paper?
- If questioned by customers – what should we say?
- What checks are put in place to stop inappropriate loans being sold?
- We have been getting calls from the press – what do we say?

Scenario 2. Breaking news

Police have cordoned off the EWB HQ in London today as a result of what is believed to be a so-called white powder attack.

Members of the emergency services in chemical suits have been seen going into the building on Liverpool Street in the City of London and a decontamination unit is on site.

Police will not say whether a toxic substance has been used or whether anyone has been injured, but no one is allowed in or out of the building.

There is speculation that this is the work of animal rights activists known as the Animal Freedom Movement (AFM).

EWB feature on the activists' website as a potential target as it provides loans to Cambridge Life Studies – the company which uses animals as part of its testing procedure.

In the last few minutes the AFM has posted a statement on its website claiming responsibility for the attack:

> *Today we have sent a clear message to all those who have connections with Cambridge Life Studies – that disgusting organization that abuses animals. We will attack anyone who profits from the misery and exploitation of fellow creatures. This is all part of our ongoing campaign. We know all about the other banks that help Cambridge Life Studies – we know who you are and your names are on our website. We never give in and we always win.*

EWB is yet to comment, but this must be having a severe impact on its ability to run its business.

Testing the plan

Injections to be used during the course of play:

Scenario 2, Injection 1

The AFM has just issued a demand on its website that EWB cease trading for 24 hours from midnight tonight. If it does not a further chemical attack is planned on another, unspecified EWB building.

Scenario 2, Injection 2

Rumours are circulating that a package containing white powder has been found at the EWB branch at Jackson Street in Newcastle. Some witnesses are saying this is another attack – the police are yet to comment.

******

This injection should be used by journalists and members of EWB staff at the Jackson Street branch.

Scenario 2, Injection 3

There are reports of two members of EWB staff at St Andrews Square being taken ill. There is immediate speculation that this is as a result of toxic chemical poisoning; some are saying it might be anthrax.

However, another cause may be the severe flu that has been affecting staff recently.

Suggested questions:

Media

Lines that reporters might be taking:

- Why is EWB being attacked?
- What is the current situation?
- Are there injuries/casualties?

Testing the plan

- What is EWB's connection with Cambridge Life Studies?
- Security? Security lapse?
- Warnings given?
- Seriousness of attack/chemical?
- Previous threats?
- Effect on business/share price?
- Blackmail?
- Push for press statement/interview.

EWB staff

Participants can play the roles of staff or family members of staff phoning in to find out:

- What is going on?
- Are people injured?
- What should they do/where should they go?
- We have been getting calls from the press – what do we say?
- What do we say to customers?
- What about security at our branch?
- Is our ability to trade damaged?
- Should we go to work today?

How the teams fared

Prior to the event participants were given an overview as to what was expected of them. Facilitators then outlined the running of the exercise. The teams took a few minutes to find their feet, but most established roles and responsibilities quickly leading to strong team cohesion.

Subsequent analysis of the press statements and briefing notes produced by the teams reflected a strong sense of corporate identity and this resulted in consistent messages from most teams. Some players felt that internal communications were handled well whereas some felt that too little information was given to the media.

Those who had to face the television camera towards the end of the exercise found it daunting, but as they were well briefed and had decided on the

Testing the plan

messages they wanted to convey, all gave a credible performance. From the players' evaluation forms it was clear they felt challenged and engaged throughout the exercise.

Action plan

It was felt that the EWB incident communications strategy lacked templates. The following were suggested:

- A template for noting calls from journalists, as well as one for media monitoring, and pre-prepared press statements covering a broad range of issues
- Key messages and facts should be prominently displayed in the communications room so that press enquiries could be answered quickly
- It was judged that there needed to be a more formal recording of information flow – teams made only a limited effort to record events, timings and decisions.

I want to stage a similar exercise – is there anything else I need to know?

The news scenarios are key to this type of exercise. For maximum impact, make sure the organization involved is either to blame for something or – rightly or wrongly – perceived to be to blame. This will allow for rigorous questioning from the press.

Here are some pointers:

- An exercise of this type will either be run by, or in conjunction with, a senior press officer – if it is the latter make sure you work with them on the planning, particularly on creating and writing the news scenarios
- Keep the participants focused and do not let the timetable slip. Ensure you have enough facilitators to move the teams promptly from one scenario to the next
- Prepare evaluation forms and insist that they are completed
- Bring all the participants together at the completion of the exercise and get a spokesperson from each team to talk for no more than five minutes about how their team fared

Communication Strategies

Testing the plan

- If the exercise takes place in the morning, remember to provide lunch for everyone – they will be tired and hungry.

> *What have I learned from this chapter?*
> - Plans need to be tested to prove their worth
> - Exercise categories reflect the scale of involvement and planning effort required
> - The type of exercise chosen will be driven by its aims and objectives
> - High-level management endorsement of all aspects of an exercise is essential.

14. Communication plan checklist

'When a dog bites a man that is not news, but when a man bites a dog that is news.' Charles Anderson Dana

Time to get cracking

You have read the book, now it is time for you to start writing or updating your incident communication plan. To help keep you on track here is a checklist of elements you will require.

Call out

- Communications team call out, including names and all contact details
- Contact details for other key staff who may need to be reached or kept informed
- A designated individual must be tasked with keeping these details up to date
- In larger companies a call-cascade system will be required.

The plan

- Statement of intent
- Roles and responsibilities for all communications team members and other staff need to be assigned
- Identify a chief spokesperson and deputy
- These individuals need to receive media training
- Identify the head of communications
- Media staff who will handle both internal and external communications – including press releases, holding statements and 'lines to take'
- Press officers who will talk directly to the press and other stakeholders including customers and suppliers
- An ability to update constantly the CEO and other executives
- Call-takers (may need to be drafted in from other departments)
- Templates for call-takers
- Media monitors (in house or outsourced)
- Templates for media monitors

Communication plan checklist

- Approval procedures and mechanisms for all communications team output (holding statements, press releases, 'lines to take', etc.)
- Pre-prepared press releases and holding statements
- The ability to run the communications room on a 24/7 basis
- An aide-mémoire to support the communications team at the outset of an incident
- Identify a note-taker or secretary to record all major decisions and events.

Fact sheets and information

- Company fact sheets
- Contact numbers for emergency services
- Contact numbers for other key stakeholders – customers, suppliers, media, hospitals
- Contact details of third-party experts who might speak on the organization's behalf
- Information on past crises
- Details of recovery site
- Website access
- Possible dark website to be activated when incident starts.

Resources

- A budget
- Extra phone lines/computers/mobile phones, etc.
- Other resources as required (including people, equipment and office space)
- Staff/contractors who may be required during an emergency.

Media

- Best practice for dealing with the media in an emergency
- Co-ordinate the response to media requests and enquiries
- Ensure prompt action of media requests
- Ensure consistency of messages
- Stay in touch with the public mood
- Continually update media contacts
- Provide adequate back-up for spokespeople
- Develop appropriate Q&As

Communication plan checklist

- Ensure the communications room is the media's first call for information
- Press conferences – where should they be held and best practice for holding them
- Press packs (including pictures).

Public information

- Manage response to the public's request for information
- Set up emergency information telephone service, if appropriate
- Manage public information websites.

Stakeholder information

- Arrange for information to be disseminated to other stakeholders
- Respond to their requests.

Finally

- Your communications plan must work within and complement your business continuity plan
- The plan must dovetail with *BS 25999 Business Continuity Management*.

Good luck!

References

1. Ratner, G. *The Rise and Fall ... and Rise Again*, Capstone, 2007

2. http://www.telegraph.co.uk/news/uknews/1358985/Sept-11-a-good-day-to-bury-bad-news.html

3. http://ppa.sagepub.com/cgi/content/abstract/17/4/39